CUSTOMER SERVICE IS JUST FOREPLAY

THE MODERN CUSTOMER EXPERIENCE WILL SEPARATE YOU FROM YOUR COMPETITION

JASON D. CASS
BRIAN APPLETON

© 2015 Cappleton
5600 Ashworth Rd
West Des Moines, IA 50266

WRITTEN FOR
INSURANCE
AGENTS

BY
INSURANCE
AGENTS

"Thank you for buying this book and entrusting me with your money, time and energy, I am grateful you made that investment with me today. My highest purpose is to insure that you are successful.

In keeping with that purpose I have put together additional resources and tools only available to the readers of this book. Please visit insuranceforeplay.com/ resources and insuranceforeplay.com/tools and enter your email to get free access to these special programs. Here you will learn about the online tools and strategies that myself and other agents use.

Also, I would be very grateful if you would be so kind as to leave a review for this book on Amazon once you are done reading. Here is where I would say good luck, but you won't need luck now that you have this book!

Enjoy and god bless."

JASON D. CASS

Praise for the Book

"Customer Service is Just Foreplay is a tremendous "road map" for insurance agents to move beyond just providing excellent customer service, but rather, a complete customer experience. The combination of real-world applications and examples, coupled with digital strategies and recommendations, make this a go-to resource for any insurance agent to survive and thrive in years to come."

Carrie Reynolds - "The Insurance Goddess"

Owner & Agent
Alan Galvez Insurance

"There is no one in the independent insurance industry as dialed-in to the marketing struggles of the everyday agent like Jason Cass. Customer Service Is Just Foreplay speaks the language of the agent from the agent's perspective. If you want to grow your agency in the digital world we live in today, do what Jason tells you."

Ryan Hanley, CIC

Digital Marketing Lead for TrustedChoice.com
Founder of Hanley Media Lab

"Jason has taken all of his wisdom, which has made him one of the top thought leaders of the insurance industry, and put it in this book. The tools that he gives you will help propel your agency into the future, because without them, your agency won't survive. He then takes it one step further by demonstrating that it's no longer about customer service, but about the customer experience. Take these words to heart and be the agent you've always wanted to be."

Joshua Lipstone

Vice President
ISU-Lipstone Insurance Group

"This book is the next evolution in what agencies should be doing to compete in today's online world. Jason's ideas mixed with Brian's writing style and structure give you a defined strategy any agent can apply to their business."

Doug Reichardt

Retired CEO & Chairman
Holmes Murphy & Associates

Praise for the Author

"Jason Cass is electric, energetic, and quite honestly, he's contagious. People want to know what he will say and do next.

I've seen him take a room full of people at seven in the morning and get them excited and rejuvenated about their jobs and our industry. The best part about him is his ability to take a complex subject and have everyone not only understand it, but embrace it.

Many people have great ideas, but Jason Cass focuses only on those that are viable, dependable, proven and effective. When you meet him, or study his ideas, you will know this is a man that has no time for anything less."

Boyd McGehee

President
Talladega Insurance Agency

"Hold on tight! Listening to Jason Cass can feel like being on Mr. Toad's Wild Ride. Jason is passionate about this industry and cares about its future. You can see that passion come out every time he gives a presentation at an association or vendor event.

Jason and I connected via social media several years ago and have become good friends. I have watched him become one of the most respected advocates in insurance. Without question, Jason is a thought leader and a respected representative of the new generation of insurance agents."

Rick Morgan

Owner
Rick Morgan Consulting

"Jason uses his rare talents to the fullest extent, taking advantage of customer experience technology improvements to provide the type of service people expect while delivering added touches that set him, and our industry, apart.

Jason is unique not only In the way he clearly understands the WHY of these critical process improvements, but he also gets the HOW. This makes his insights valuable to any agent."

Ron Berg

Executive Director
Agents Council for Technology

Patron Acknowledgement

Thank you to the following companies that helped make this dream a reality.

QQ Solutions

Insurance Agent Mobile App

Marble Box

Agency Multiplied

Thomas H. Wetzel & Associates

Simply Easier Payments, Inc.

INDUSTRY PROFESSIONAL THANK YOU PAGE

Thank you to the following people who always leave me inspired.

Ryan Hanley	Brent Kelly	Jim Schubert
Chris Paradiso	Carrie Reynolds	Joey Giangola
John Carroll	Rick Morgan	Steve Anderson
Ron Berg	Tom Wetzel	Chris Amrhein
	Claudia Rossberg McClain	

Without your guidance and energy, this book would not be possible. These people have broken down barriers and pushed the envelope from the very beginning. Thank you for all you do for this industry.

PERSONAL THANK YOU PAGE

God, thank you for giving me the gift of potential. It's a gift I intend to use.

To my wife, nobody has made me a better person than you.

Mike Beard, you have meant more to me as a mentor than you could ever know. You mean a great deal to my family and friends, and you've made me a better family member and friend. You showed me how to respect and recognize greatness in others, and you showed me how to find it in myself. Thank you.

Ryan Hanley, I see you as a giant. Whenever I feel weak, intimidated, or unsure, I know that I can contact you to remind me that I am not alone in this odyssey of helping others GROW their business by gaining attention online. As you have said, it is "Content Warfare." We've started great things together, and I'm excited to see what's next.

Finally, a special thank you to my friend and former colleague, Brian Appleton, for helping me transfer the ideas in my head on to the pages of this book. Your contributions in writing and structuring my strategies have been invaluable.

To anyone else who has helped and accepted me as I am, thank you. That means more than anything.

Contents

Introduction

Section 1

Section 2

Closing

FOREWORD

"It's hard to do something different, especially when you've experienced some success and are comfortable with the way you do business. When we looked at the road ahead, and the distance we needed to go to get there, the one thing harder to do than change was to sit on the sidelines and do nothing.

There's been a big shift in the way today's consumer assigns value and makes buying decisions. We knew we had to take a hard look at our agency if we wanted to stay relevant for years to come. Getting the entire team on board wasn't easy at first. Many were content with the status quo.

Once we expressed where the ship was headed, everyone either aligned with our vision or moved on to do what was best for both of us. Thus began our journey in implementing the strategies laid out in this book -- transforming good customer service into a great Customer Experience.

Since beginning the process, we have seen significant improvements in our ability to turn high quality leads into customers as well as improve the overall profitability of our agency. We can now sleep peacefully at night knowing our agency has a secure and prosperous plan for the future.

Jason has been ahead of the game for years and helped us stay competitive. He is a knowledgeable and trusted resource to help you improve your ROI and profitability. This book redefines industry tactics for the better and ensures a sustainable future. We encourage you to take what you learn here to heart."

Grady Gamble & Greg Rogers

Owners
Golden Rule Insurance

1

Seeing What
the Travel Agent
Never Saw

Imagine you're a child in the 1950s who just attended their first big circus with mom and dad. Huge, exotic animals from all over the world are doing amazing stunts right in front of you. The smells, sounds, and pageantry are beyond anything you've ever witnessed.

As you watch, a wide-eyed child full of wonderment, your dad puts his arm around your shoulders and says, "Isn't this show amazing?" You nod your head in agreement. He then leans in and says something that leaves you questioning everything you just saw.

"Forty years from now, the circus will be nothing like this. There will be no animals -- only people, music, and acrobats. This new circus will be the most popular and expensive one on the planet, and the act you saw today will struggle to survive. Can you imagine?"

One of our greatest human limitations is our inability to see things for other than how they are. In 1983, there was no concept of a circus without animals. A year later, two gentleman by the name of Guy Lalibertéand and Gilles Ste-Croix created one -- Cirque du Soleil.

In the insurance industry, the competition is inventing a circus without any animals. Don't be the Ringling Brothers, standing around thinking you have the best show on earth.

It's not a question of *if* but *when* the industry will change. If you've been an agent for more than a decade, did you ever think what has happened to personal lines was possible 15 years ago?

There are four major challenges facing the industry right now.

New Competition with Better Tools - A gluttony of

3

competition has entered the marketplace. Household names like Amazon, Google and Wal-Mart are now offering insurance solutions. Mark Cuban just invested over a million dollars in a comparative rater startup any consumer can use. Zenefits, a startup that simplifies that complexity of health benefits, became one of the quickest companies to ever raise $100 million in venture capital.

The key to our longevity is owning, and maintaining, a robust percentage of the industry's market share. If you're not working for it, there's a great deal of business out there for anyone to grab, and I mean anyone. Your competition knows this well, and they're swarming like sharks who see blood.

New and Emerging Technology - Technology has completely shifted how consumers buy and perceive value. The Internet is now the main hub to get information on insurance. The problem is that not enough agents are embracing online platforms, or they're using them incorrectly.

Becoming the Disposable Middle-Man - Insurance companies are looking for ways to dodge agents and go directly to customers. Many have started reducing commissions while others are being forced out altogether. Technology has made your job disposable unless you use it to your advantage. If we don't give insurance companies a good reason to keep us around, they may decide not to one day.

Losing 50 Percent of the Industry - Many agents ask me, "Why should I care if 50 percent of the insurance industry is retiring or leaving in the next five years? That means more business for me." Insurance agencies need to work together, not against each other. If we don't seek out new talent and capabilities necessary to create a sustainable future for this industry, our buying power as a whole is going to severely diminish.

To elaborate on the points above, there is a report by McKinsey & Company titled, "Agent of The Future: The Evolution of Property and Casualty Insurance Distribution." It's one of the most eye-opening pieces the industry has received in the last 20 years. The report goes extensively into how our industry is changing and what agents need to do to stay ahead of the curve. Here is a glimpse at what's mentioned:

- Most personal lines and small commercial consumers will interact with carriers and agents through multiple channels -- such as in-person, on mobile devices, by phone, Internet and video conferencing.

- Agents will only be compensated for the unique value they deliver to the customer and the carrier.

- Successful agents will deliver tailored customer expertise and excel at multi-channel marketing while widening their scale and operational efficiency.

- Carriers will continue to use technology to increase direct interaction with the customer at a lower cost.

- Customers no longer recognize their agent as the source of their insurance. Brand names with big advertising budgets are more recognizable.

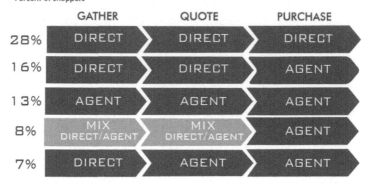

AUTO INSURANCE CUSTOMERS ARE USING
MORE CHANNELS IN THEIR SHOPPING JOURNEY

Top 5 multichannel shopping journeys*
Percent of shoppers

	GATHER	QUOTE	PURCHASE
28%	DIRECT	DIRECT	DIRECT
16%	DIRECT	DIRECT	AGENT
13%	AGENT	AGENT	AGENT
8%	MIX DIRECT/AGENT	MIX DIRECT/AGENT	AGENT
7%	DIRECT	AGENT	AGENT

Source: 2012 McKinsey Auto Insurance Customer Insights Research

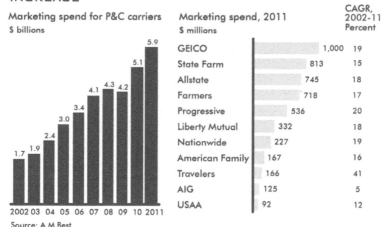

U.S. P&C MARKETING SPEND CONTINUES TO
INCREASE

Marketing spend for P&C carriers
$ billions

Year	Spend
2002	1.7
03	1.9
04	2.4
05	3.0
06	3.4
07	4.1
08	4.3
09	4.2
10	5.1
2011	5.9

Source: A M Best

Marketing spend, 2011 $ millions		CAGR, 2002-11 Percent
GEICO	1,000	19
State Farm	813	15
Allstate	745	18
Farmers	718	17
Progressive	536	20
Liberty Mutual	332	18
Nationwide	227	19
American Family	167	16
Travelers	166	41
AIG	125	5
USAA	92	12

In short, McKinsey & Company offers an analytical and objective view of what's ahead. One thing that stood out to me was the author's comparison of travel agents and insurance agents.

For those too young to remember, there was a time when most travel plans were made through a travel agent. Now with online services like Expedia and Orbitz, agents have dropped off like flies. Those who survived had to transform. Similarly, successful insurance agents will be those who choose to evolve.

AIRLINE BOOKINGS THROUGH TRADITIONAL TRAVEL AGENTS DECLINED PRECIPITOUSLY WITH THE ADVENT OF INTERNET BOOKING TOOLS

U.S. airline leisure and unmanaged business sales by channel

Percent

	1999	2005	2010	2013F	
Total	100	100	100	100	
Airline Website		22	34	37	
Online Travel Agency	95 (3/2)	12	16	13	
Offline*		66	50	50	

*Includes traditional travel agencies (the majority), airline call centers and airport sales.

Source: PhoCusWright; US Online Travel Overview reports

THE NUMBER OF TRADITIONAL TRAVEL AGENTS DROPPED, BUT THOSE THAT REMAIN ARE LARGER AND MORE SUCCESSFUL

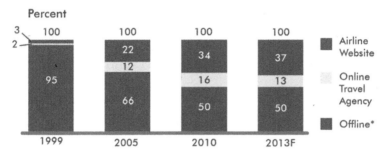

	1995	2000	2011
Number of traditional travel agencies*	47,000	38,800	14,000
Air sales per location $ million	1.6	2.2	5.8
Total air sales $ billion	73.0	83.5	82.1

*Airline Reporting Corporation (ARC) accredited agencies - those that are able to issue air tickets

Source: PhoCusWright; ARC; ASTA.org

7

J.D. Power and Associates named Geico as having the best customer service among millennials. An appropriate honor given the company's success in reaching this group of early technology adopters whose attention spans are considerably shorter than their Baby Boomer predecessors. With customer expectations increasingly centered on saving time and money, online companies that deliver these coveted attributes will continue to thrive.

Despite the challenges ahead, this book is not meant to deter you, but to help you progress. The forthcoming information will adequately prepare you to transform how you do business in order to keep pace with advancements that will continue to be common place with your customers.

2

THE
GROUND
RULES

The enemy of being the best is not being the worst. It's being mediocre. Motivational speaker, Zig Ziglar, once said it like this, "If you put a pot on the stove and bring it to a boil, and then put a frog in the pot, the frog will instantly jump out knowing the water is way too hot to survive."

In contrast, if you put a pot of cold water on the stove and put the frog in while slowly turning up the heat, something much different happens. The frog will swim around obliviously until it meets its cruel fate. You are that frog, and consumers are turning up the heat.

I've been an insurance agent for more than 14 years, interacting with everyone from the top to the bottom of this industry. I know how you operate, think, and react when you're told something you don't want to hear.

Many mean well, but few actually have what it takes to keep steady with the industry's shifting landscape. If you fall into this group, it's time to pull yourself up or else you'll be on your way down.

Implementing every idea in this book is a lot to digest, no matter the size or profitability of your business. That shouldn't be your goal. Your goal is to read this book with an open mind and then decide which strategies work best. You don't have to do it alone either. I'll show you how to recruit others to be a part of your customer experience team.

You worked hard to build what you have, right? This won't be nearly as hard as when you first started out, but it will take work. Embracing and applying new ideas is exciting but also uncomfortable and a little scary. The best thing you can do for your professional self is step out of your comfort zone and ignite growth.

This book is meant to serve as a study guide for understanding and reaching today's customer. Read it thoroughly to effectively implement the information in the pages that follow.

One size does not fit all.

Customer Service Is Just Foreplay was written so any agent or agency, regardless of the business' size, experience, or geographical location, could internalize its contents and put it to use. I've provided a framework of best practices that will help you identify areas for improvement within your marketing process. Every organization has a different set of needs and priorities. You decide what is best for you.

The tools mentioned here were strategically picked for the *Modern Customer Experience*.

Over the last few years, I've had the opportunity to speak at associations, vendor events and insurance companies across the country. On nearly every occasion, agents want to know what tools and services I use. In order to help you personalize your customer experience, I reached out to several companies whose products I've found to be invaluable. In return, they agreed to offer discounted prices, reduced and/or waived sign-up fees, and program bonuses available exclusively to readers. While the products mentioned below aren't the only ones on the market, numerous agents (myself included) have had great results.

- Agency Management System QQCatalyst® from QQ Solutions

- Insurance Agent Mobile Application

- Simply Easier Payments Payment Processing Program

- Simply Easier ACORD Forms' Self Service Certificates Program

- Rocket Referrals Outsourced Referral Programs

- Marble Box Agency Operations Outsourcing Services

- Agency Multiplied Commercial Quoting Program

- Tom H. Wetzel and Associates Social Media Content Roadmap

You can access a complete list of partner products by visiting www.insuranceforeplay.com/tools and entering your email address. I encourage you to bookmark the website and refer back to it, even after you've finished the book, as industry tools are added.

There are step-by-step strategies on creating a better customer experience not mentioned in this book.

I've put together a wealth of additional information for you outside of the pages of this book as well. Visit the Resource Library by going to www.insuranceforeplay. com/resources and entering your email address. There are valuable strategies available now, and in the months to come, that any agent can apply to creating a *Modern Customer Experience*. Here are just some of the content pieces in motion:

- How creating relationships with local real estate agents can help you generate 3-5 leads a month with an 80 percent closing ratio.

- The first three chapters of Ryan Hanley's book, "Content Warfare - How to Tell Your Story, Build Your Audience, and Win the Battle for Attention," absolutely free.

- How to run a 12 day Facebook contest that creates $40,000 in revenue. I actually did this for an agency in Arkansas, and I'll tell you exactly how I made it happen.

- How to create your own state-of-the-art video studio for as little as $250 dollars.

- Fillable forms I built and use that follow and simplify the ACORD forms.

- Excellent referral process any agent can apply to their business.

- Rocket Referrals eBook on referrals titled, "The Agents' Guide to Referrals: How to Implement a Profitable Referral Strategy for Your Insurance Agency," absolutely free.

No one expects you to recreate your business tomorrow. Some things take time and practice. You didn't write all of your big accounts on the very first day. There was a lot you had to learn and try before you found what worked. By the time you're done reading this book, you should have identified one or two things you can implement now. Store the rest for when you're ready to take the next step.

This book is divided into two parts. The first discusses the foundation for building the *Modern Customer Experience*. Before you can focus on sales, marketing, and quoting, you have to have the right strategies and tools in place. We'll get started by going over things like your agency management system, website, customer self-service, mobile applications and payments.

The second section focuses on the sales funnel, marketing and lead generation. We'll also discuss building conversion machines and the technology platforms you can use to create more efficiencies for your business. In addition, I'll assist you with establishing an automated process as well as improving customer retention, satisfaction and cross-selling. You'll learn how to increase profits by streamlining these elements into a seamless, internal process.

The infographic in section two will guide you through my entire approach along with the color coded chapters that allow you to easily track where you left off.

Before we get started; take a deep breath and relax! I know this seems like a lot, but we'll take it one step at a time.

3

CUSTOMER ~~SERVICE~~ EXPERIENCE

I'll never forget the moment I realized the insurance industry would never be the same. I was on the phone with a potential customer doing my usual discovery process when she said, "You local agents don't provide the same customer service Geico does."

I immediately felt defensive. I couldn't believe she thought such a thing, let alone said it to me. I had all the markets she could ever want, and I was right down the street. I had the best coverages and always faxed or emailed customers certificates as soon as they were requested. I always answered customer calls. I did everything a customer could want. There was no way in hell Geico offered better customer service than me. I asked her why she felt that way, and her response made me see things in a whole new light.

"I can do everything online with Geico. They have a chat feature and a mobile app. I can access my insurance card and make payments online any time I want to."

Although this woman initially used the words "customer service," what she really meant was that Geico was giving her a customer experience. Customer needs and desires had changed right in front of me, and I was no longer in a position to dictate how people should do business with me.

Do you know how often coverage comes into play for the customer? CarInsurance.com cited that a customer will have a car accident about once every 18 years. According to Zack's Investment Research, it's about once every 10 years for homeowner's insurance. Depending on the industry, some commercial lines customers may file claims more frequently, but it's highly sporadic and volatile. Do you want the only real interactions you have with your client to be when something bad happens to them? Though a claim lets you show your true value, what happens if someone goes a year with no claims? How

16

do you show your value? The truth is there are plenty of other times to make meaningful connections with your customers throughout the year.

It is so ingrained in us to master coverages, limits, and service that we think it's all people care about, but it's not. When I speak at state associations or industry events I ask, "What makes you better than your competition?" Eighty percent of the room would say it was their customer service. The other 20 percent would say it's their marketing (which really means their insurance markets).

Here is the problem with our idea of customer service. What you perceive to be a competitive advantage is what customers now think of as a standard level of service. It's what they expect as a part of their premium. It doesn't separate you from other agents. Providing a customer experience is about how the consumer of today perceives value and makes buying decisions. **It's about the interactions a customer has with you and/or your agency throughout the life of your business relationship.**

A customer experience is about convenience and integrating digital and social platforms into your marketing plan. It's about being online and staying connected to the consumer at all times; communicating in ways they prefer, not the way you prefer. Everything comes together in the marketing, prospecting, communication, selling, servicing, retention and cross-selling process. **The *Modern Customer Experience* means offering tangible products, like an agency mobile app, e-signatures, self service, online quoting and online payments, that go through you instead of the insurance company.**

As agents, we like to say the hardest thing about selling insurance is that it's intangible. That isn't true anymore. Everything I just mentioned is tangible. Digital platforms

17

are common place. We need to stop talking about good customer service and start talking about a great customer experience. Providing customers with tangible technology solutions helps bridge this gap, but there is still more to explore.

People crave experiences. The best companies go beyond their product or service to give people an experience that identifies with their lifestyle. At McDonald's, for instance, I know almost everything on their menu is bad for me, but I still buy fast food from time to time.

Why?

Consistency.

No matter where I go to get a Big Mac, it'll be the same Big Mac I could get at any other McDonald's. There is no variance. I always know what I'm in for.

Some agents struggle with offering too much variance. What happens if a customer needs to access a certificate over the weekend? Can they get it from an app? What if they need to make a payment? Can they do it through you, or are you forcing them to pay through the insurance company? Aren't you giving the insurance company one more reason to cut you out of the equation? Aren't you putting the consumer in a situation where they question why they need you at all?

Our value as agents has shifted. Before you're successful building a customer experience, you have to stop dwelling on what used to work. If you don't understand the consumer of today, and five years from now, you'll never be as effective or successful as the agent who does.

Evolutionist Charles Darwin said, "It is not the strongest of the species that survives, nor the most intelligent, but the one most responsive to change."

We are going through a new form a Darwinism -- Digital Darwinism. Brian Solis, award winning author and speaker, described Digital Darwinism as "the phenomenon when technology and society evolve faster than an organization can adapt. Every fabric of a company is strained due to internal and external influences. The challenge lies amongst the very leaders running the show. Their mission, and the processes and systems they support, may already be working against them."

Think about the last part for a second. The things you're doing now may actually be working against you. Is what you're doing today giving you the same results you got five or ten years ago? If your business is growing with a dying demographic, aren't you just speeding up the death of your business too?

The truth is that customer service, as many agents know it, is just foreplay. It doesn't do much to satisfy or keep people around for the long-haul anymore. The agents who come out on top will be those who are most responsive to new ideas.

SECTION 1

*If we bring the customer of today
into the agency of yesterday,
we will have no tomorrow.*

4

Agency Management Systems that Foster Customer Experience

It's hard to believe 20 percent of agencies in the insurance industry don't have Agency Management Systems (AMS). Good agency management systems do a lot, but they do one thing above everything else. They store customer information. Agencies without an AMS will never be able to organize and use data to build better, smarter, and more cost-effective systems.

Downloading and uploading customer information into an AMS eliminates manual entry, which eliminates human error. Having a record of your customers' buying habits in one place will show you where and how your efforts are paying off.

AMS is similar to when direct bill came around. Agents were in an uproar, because they thought it cut them out of transactions. Harnessing customer data cements you between the customer and the insurance company. If you aren't keeping track of their information, it makes more sense for customers to go directly to the insurance company.

Storing information makes online payments, obtaining ID cards, answering coverage questions (deductible, limits, etc.) and claims assistance a whole lot easier for customers. You benefit too with these added conveniences:

- Have someone produce birthday cards for your customers in your own words and handwriting.

- Sell other lines of insurance automatically during renewals or any other time of service.

- Segment customers to improve communication and cross-selling.

- Communicate with customers by electronically funneling all conversations to your management system through digital platforms such as text, email and social media.

- Navigate information in a few simple clicks to provide better quotes.

- Easily administer renewals, allowing you to re-quote your customers more efficiently.

Customer expectations have changed, and agents push back because it means learning and implementing new processes. Creating an internal structure that makes customer requests seamless for both you and your client will help maintain a steady stream of revenue and create loyal customers.

Everyone, including you, wants to know they're getting the best price and value. If you really do have the most affordable coverages, wouldn't you want to consistently prove that to your customers? With the right management system, you can run a renewal quote through an agency rater (we'll address this later), take a screen capture on your computer and compare it to other prices. Then, send your customer an email with what you found. They'll appreciate that you're looking out for them.

While having an AMS is better than not having one at all, having the right one is critical. Predictable systems are critical (think McDonald's). Most management platforms allow for personalization, giving you the ability to design the system in a format that works best for you.

The best agency management systems have an open source Application Programming Interface (API). It's fairly new to our industry though others have been using it for more than a decade.

An API allows two or more different web-based software programs to work in cooperation with one another. Think dual computer monitors. The monitors work well separately, but once connected, their functionality increases allowing you to move your browser from one screen to the other. APIs operate similarly, effortlessly moving your data back and forth.

Steve Anderson, a renowned thought leader on technology in the insurance industry, described what happened when Sales Force, one of the largest CRM (Customer Relationship Management) systems in the world, made the change to an open source API.

"The SalesForce platform was only available to third party providers after paying a large fee. In 2008, they decided to provide open access to their platform (through an API) at no cost. When they made this decision, their business doubled in a very short time. They were giving their customers what they wanted, the ability to work with systems and programs, in the way they wanted and with what worked best for them."

The core strength of a software program, specifically those with an API, is managing customer information and data. You get to decide how you want to combine programs with what you're already using. For instance, let's say you find the email marketing program designed by your AMS just isn't what you need. So, you find an email marketing program that you do like and want it to work with your AMS. Attempting to have the two work together would be very expensive. So, you're either forced to use your AMS's email marketing solution or pay a hefty fee.

Steve Anderson summed this up well when he stated, "Agency management systems were created to be policy data management systems, not marketing systems. "

Agency management systems weren't designed to operate as a jack-of-all-trades. Instead, look for an AMS that will work with the tools you need for customer management and marketing. There are quite a few agency management systems to consider. Many choose systems based on price, agency size and the best overall fit for operations. Ask yourself what you need your current system to do.

RESOURCES

QQ Solutions

Throughout my years in the industry, there is one AMS that stands out from the rest. It's not just because of its API capabilities, although that is certainly important. QQCatalyst® from QQ Solutions is one of the fastest growing and flexible systems on the market. Here's why:

- Their foundation was built on collecting, organizing and sharing information between programs to give you the best of everything.

- QQ Catalyst is a truly customizable AMS.

- QQ Solutions values and listens to customer input. Though structured like a large company, they maintain a refreshing small company mentality when it comes to customer service.

- They move quickly and can make changes to products within a few weeks.

- Their system is cloud-based and runs on any device.

- In addition, QQ Catalyst works on accounting programs, which contrary to what many agents believe, is a huge benefit. Instead of forcing your accountant to use a system they're unfamiliar with, QQ Catalyst allows you to connect to QuickBooks. I can do direct/agency billing along with everything else my old agency management system could do, and it makes my life much easier.

They are easy to manage, there are no set-up fees, nothing to install, they're cost effective, and they focus on customer service. If you would like a detailed evaluation of their system, check out our resources section.

5

Curb Appeal in the Virtual World

In 2010, I decided to start my own agency out of a 56 square foot room in my basement. The size of the town I live in is nearly that small with a population of only 13,000. Quite a few people, including my wife, questioned how I was going to make it work.

The truth is that they were concerned about how I was ever going to earn people's trust. How could I build value with my prospects so they would buy? More importantly, why would they ever buy insurance from a guy running an agency out of his basement?

I wasn't worried, because I knew something they didn't. The Internet is like a huge mall, the only difference being that it allows people to browse from the comfort of their home. My website was going to serve as my virtual storefront and allow me to run my agency from any location.

Prospective and current customers will visit your website for three reasons:

1. They're looking for information on how to communicate with you. Your contact information should be visible on every page of your website, preferably in the top right so customers can easily find it.

2. They want to make a payment. You should allow your customers to make insurance payments directly on your website, so they don't feel like they have to go to the insurance company's site.

3. They need a quote. A rater is ideal for supplying quotes. If you chose not to have one, then you should supply a ready-made form for customers to fill out.

Geico's website hits all three of these points. It's why so many leisurely browsers are converted into paying customers. If their site looked terrible, they wouldn't have such luck. The majority of websites in the insurance industry are either outdated, hard to navigate, overloaded with information or have absolutely no focus on marketing.

Your website should be easy to navigate and encompass the right tools and Call to Action (CTA) to make what seems like a complex decision an easy one. It should position you as the expert while allowing you to qualify or disqualify the type of customer you want to do business with. In addition, a well-structured website will have the following elements:

Both search engines and people can easily read and navigate it

Your website's framework should be assembled so potential customers can immediately find exactly what they're looking for. It should be simple, clean and elegant. Don't overload the site with every plugin and widget out there.

Each section on your site should cover the width of the page and the words should be easily visible. The font, typography, and letter spacing can have a tremendous impact on your visitors. Images and videos should also be prominently featured. Incorporate real pictures and background information on your agency and staff, a component that's shown to be critical in customer engagement. Unlike online-only insurance companies, you have the advantage of creating personal relationships with customers. Assigning a face to a name is one extra step that'll set you apart.

Aside from being aesthetically pleasing and easy to read, your website should satisfy search engine spiders/

bots. One of the main reasons WordPress is such a great platform is because of its Search Engine Optimization (SEO) features. If you want your business to have any sort of a presence on the Internet, having a great SEO ranking is a must.

Your website also needs to be lightweight (no flash or heavy scripts) with clean, documented code. You'll want to put in a sitemap to help Google and other search engines understand exactly what you want them to crawl and index. "Crawl" and "index" simply mean search and store. When Google is crawling your site, they're searching for content to store in their archive so it can be retrieved at a later time when someone is looking you up online. Internal and external links also play a huge part in your online success. Properly incorporating and referencing outside content by using hyperlinks within your own content, found on your blog or social media sites, will help improve your search ranking.

Visible contact information and convenient customer service

Research on website optimization tells us exactly how people interact with online sites. Their eyes shift from top left to top right then diagonally back and forth down the page, just as they would reading a book. So, it makes sense for your logo and contact information to be located at the top left and right corners of your page.

People also prefer being able to chat live with customer support. A live chat feature allows online visitors to instant message customer service when they have a question or request. Customer service will then walk the potential customer through their options or help them find a solution. If you already have someone designated to handle customer service calls, this should be a standard feature on your site.

An appropriate and well-positioned Call-To-Action (CTA)

Your website should be designed with the goal of converting visitors into prospects and prospects into customers. You're only afforded a small window of opportunity for a visitor to take action, so show them what you want them to do and where they can do it.

Start by deciding what it is that you want your visitors to do. Do you want them to call you? Do you want them to ask for a quote? Would you like to obtain their email address or other contact information so you can start sending your marketing campaigns directly to their inbox? What's your CTA?

Decide on a clear strategy and build a plan around it. Here are a few CTA's I've found to be highly beneficial.

Capture the prospect's email

Most people will stay on your site for less than 30 seconds before moving on. You really can judge a book by its cover. Make sure you quickly capture the visitor's contact information before they leave, so you can continue to build your relationship on other platforms.

To effectively capture an email address, offer something of high value in exchange for their information. White papers or eBooks are great options. In addition, most email marketing services have a function that allows you to integrate an email capture right onto your site.

Allow prospects to get a quote

Some agents hate the idea of offering their prospects a quote online, but it's like that old saying, "If you won't do it, someone else will." Providing quotes through your website should be done for two reasons.

1. It gets your prices out there. Sometimes, that's all people really want.

2. Even if a quote isn't completed, most systems will capture contact information so you can follow up. That is one more opportunity you didn't have before.

At the very least, you should have a "Request a Quote" button that leads your potential customer to a short form they can fill out, so you can call them at a later time and work up a quote.

Customers can make payments

Imagine the following scenario. A customer walks into your office with cash in hand and says, "I want to pay for my insurance this month." You tell them no. That's essentially what happens every time a customer comes to your website to make a payment, and you redirect them to the insurance company's website instead.

Making people take extra steps just to make a simple policy payment causes friction in customer relationships. Trust me when I say your competition isn't doing this to their customers. There is technology available now that allows you to accept customer payments on your website for no fee. This option needs to be displayed proudly on your website's homepage.

+ **More to come on this in chapter eight.**

Build in social media buttons

When structured properly, your website is a great tool for driving people to your social networks. Twitter has 232 million users, while Facebook comes in at a staggering 1.35 billion. These networks have become preferred methods of communicating and connecting for many, giving you additional channels to reach potential customers. Display your social buttons (Facebook, LinkedIn and YouTube) in a way that is easy to see and select.

Once someone leaves your website, they won't come back unless it's to contact you about an issue, make a payment or request a quote. However, they may still want to stay connected to you and vice versa. Having a social presence and incorporating social buttons into your theme is vital for making that happen. It's similar to when you exchange information with someone after you meet, so you can stay connected and hopefully meet again.

Add a blog

To be noticed by others online, Google must notice you first. Adding a useful blog to your website can really boost your search engine ranking. Whatever you choose to write about in your blog is what Google indexes. When people find your blog on other social networks, it builds your credibility as a thought leader in the industry. Your blog is the voice of your website. Teach it to sing.

Your blog posts should be easy to read, short, and contain quality content for your prospects and customers. Give people the opportunity to talk to you about your blog, and distribute it too, through social sharing buttons and a comments section.

Optimize your website for any mobile device (responsive)

With more and more people consuming digital content on mobile devices and tablets, the demand for optimized (responsive) websites has skyrocketed. A responsive website is intelligently coded on the backend to conform to any mobile device or tablet, making content easier to view and scroll through.

33

Responsive design has exploded over the past few years, and it's only going to further evolve. There are currently 241 million mobile phones in the U.S. According to a comScore study, over 50 percent of insurance shopping is done on mobile devices. Of that, 68 percent of visitors will leave a site if it isn't responsive on their phone. Designing your website for mobile optimization isn't a luxury, it's a necessity.

It's time to stop thinking of your website as a digital business card and start thinking of it as a customer conversion system. Having a great looking website with no conversion strategy is like building your agency on a deserted island. It may seem great to you, but it doesn't mean much if no one can get to it. A website is one of the most important tools your agency has. If used properly, it can turn opportunities into leads and leads into paying customers.

6

Technology When Your Customers Want it

Imagine a large elevator with a desk in it. That's my office. Whenever I'm on a webinar, video call or send a picture of it to another agent, they are blown away that I'm able to run my business in such a compact area.

You don't need much to start and run a virtual agency. I use little more than a laptop, tablet, landline phone (VOIP), smartphone, and dual printer scanner. The tools I use in my agency can be applied to anyone's, whether you have an abundance of or limited resources.

To build the *Modern Customer Experience*, you need to think differently about how customers are brought on and serviced. Start leveraging technology to get back more time and become more efficient. Here are the things to get right for a more profitable book and agency.

Risk Management Solutions

Lower profitability on accounts, because of things like lower commissions and increased operating expenses, isn't depleting customer expectations.

Though some agents feel they have less time, energy, money and resources than they did before, your commercial clients still expect you to do more to not only earn their business but to keep it. Agents must continuously evaluate how they can add value and, more importantly, profitability to their customers' bottom line.

An effective way to accomplish this is to give your customers risk management solutions that require minimal involvement on your behalf once they're implemented. Though many agents don't realize it, there are tools available online or through mobile applications.

These tools can be afforded through co-op dollars with your insurance company, by you, or your customer. No matter how you make them available, agents who can position themselves as trusted advisors instead of just taking orders will have more longevity in the industry.

Agents who focus on the *Modern Customer Experience* strategically find ways to help their clients with risk management solutions while adding profitability to their company throughout the year, not just with premiums at the end of it.

Small Commercial Lines Automation

As automation continues to progress, the next obvious evolution is the transition from personal lines to small commercial lines. There are plenty of reasons why this will happen and is happening now.

1. As driverless cars become a mainstream commodity, they'll be created smaller and safer to keep the people who operate them safe.

2. Personal auto may disappear altogether as transportation changes.

3. Prices are now more uniform, neutralizing the advantages an agent once held in BOP policies, general liability, surety bonds, etc.

Small commercial lines are ripe for disruption.

Insurance companies already get this. It's why they're always talking about small commercial. They want you to create a diverse book of commercial because it helps them do the same.

Efficient operating platforms are essential given the fear of carriers completely cutting out local agents. The push back of, "...but I provide great customer service," won't work soon. Not to mention, it's never really been the case with small commercial insurance and premiums. When you do spend time on these policies, it's as a courtesy because customer loyalty sometimes means losing money.

The margins on small commercial lines won't change much, but access to automated processing will. The best solutions will reinforce the agency model while, at the same time, giving you the tools you need to be successful in a digital world.

This is the *Modern Customer Experience*.

Customer Certificate Self Service

Self-service is a software solution for your website that gives customers the ability to access their account, certificates, and other information. It's a great option for decent-sized agencies that reissue a lot of certs.

It gives your customers access to what they need whenever they need it, and you have total control over the entire process. You never want to be the bottleneck in your customers' business. At no time can your customer fill out and print a certificate that you don't want.

These programs serve as an after-hours call center where people can review policy information, request changes and report a First Notice of Loss. Most importantly, it's added value for your customer during a disaster.

It may take a little training with your customers, and it certainly won't happen overnight, but it will improve your workflow and save you a lot of time. As commissions are reduced and expenses increased, this is one way to save money and increase profits. Every customer may not use it today, but in five years, they will.

RESOURCES

Agency Multiplied

Agency Multiplied is working hard to make sure agents remain a vital part of the small commercial lines landscape. They're currently beta-testing a free commercial lines software plugin that will live directly on an agents' website. This virtual-salesman will quote, underwrite, bind, issue and record small commercials lines policies around the clock, allowing visitors to use it after business hours and on weekends.

The plugin includes several APIs that eliminate duplicate entries with your Agency Management System, accounting software, and other programs. Their software also comes with upgrades where agents can custom configure their carrier's underwriting for complete control over the small commercial lines book.

Simply Easier ACORD Forms' Self-Service Certificates

The best service for some of your customers may be accountable self-service. Simply Easier ACORD Forms' Self-Service certificate management keeps your customers happy, with less work for you, and lets you control and track all issued certificates.

Customers can only change the certificate holder -- not limits, dates or coverages. All self-service changes are emailed to you in real time. All self-service certificates are permanently logged for your review and protection.

Cap Dat ACORD works the same on your desktop, laptop, tablet or smartphone. Allow your customers to access their information whenever and wherever.

7

Go Mobile or Get Gone

The next time you're in a crowded place, look around at what everyone is doing. Chances are they're all on their smartphones.

In the report, *Mobile in Insurance Beyond Personal Lines: Current Trends and Expectations,* Novarica Principal Karlyn Carnahan said 70 percent of property casualty insurers predict they will offer mobile capabilities. In addition, directs and carriers already have mobile apps, and they're using them to collect customer data.

Here are some other overwhelming statistics:

- In a recent survey, 70 percent of agents indicated they see value in having an agency app.

- Pew Research reports that 68 percent of Americans now use a smartphone or tablet to access the Internet.

- Eighty six percent of mobile users use apps to find or do what they need while only 14 percent use the web.

This growing demographic shares no commonalities in age, race, social status or sex. All that matters is if you are connected or unconnected. Ryan Hanley, Head of Marketing for TrustedChoice.com, coined that phrase. I think it's brilliant. Being connected verse unconnected means nothing more than whether or not you use technology in your daily life. Here are a few questions to help you determine if you're connected.

- Have you ever bought anything online?

- Have you booked a flight or vacation online?

- Do you have a smartphone, Kindle, iPad or other tablet?

- Do you read books using a digital device?

41

- Are you on a social network like Facebook, LinkedIn or Pinterest?

- Do you use Netflix? Have you watched a tv show or movie on a mobile device?

- Do you use Google?

- Do you pay your bills online?

People are no longer confined to desktop computers, because they're carrying mini computers in their pockets. Over the coming years, when customers interact with companies, they'll be reaching for their mobile devices. Businesses from every industry are taking advantage of it. Consumers are being conditioned to use their smartphones by other industries, such as banking and finance. Now insurance companies, and your competition, are using mobile applications too.

Consumers are no longer concerned about coming to our offices and meeting our people like they used to be. Some insurance companies are even bypassing agents who aren't willing to offer mobile solutions and are going straight to customers. If that doesn't scare you, it should.

Your website, mobile-optimized (responsive) website, and mobile app will each appear differently on your phone. Mobile apps are a great way for you to stay engaged with current customers and own some digital real estate. Apps also help with cross-selling, referrals, and customer loyalty.

I've had multiple customers tell me how handy it is to have my app during inopportune times. For example, when they used the app to get their information after being pulled over and their insurance card was at home. Or, simply appreciating the fact they can access certificate information any time. These are called "mobile moments," a term coined by Steve Anderson. Some other moments you can create include offering easy payments and allowing customers to make policy changes.

This industry was built on the human need to have control when life events happen that are out of our control. Having a front facing platform that addresses this need quickly and easily should be a standard in your agency.

Mobile is also a great marketing channel for automated text messages. Now I understand some agents don't want to annoy customers with additional texts, but with any marketing plan, there is a right and wrong way to do it. For instance, a text message about an upcoming payment is valuable to all parties.

The best agency mobile applications allow you to send notifications too. To reach your customers on their mobile devices without sending a text, notifications will appear on the phone's home screen after they're pushed out by the app. Before you scoff at this, think about it for a second. We may not communicate through email in the future if it can be done through cell numbers and notifications. That doesn't mean the content will disappear. It'll just be delivered in a different way.

I know agents all over the country who have great success with text message marketing and notifications. While it'll likely evolve in coming years, it is here to stay. Make collecting cell phone numbers a staple part of your intake process. If you're not sure whether your customers want to receive text notifications and messages, just ask. People aren't afraid to say they don't want something.

RESOURCES

Insurance Agent App

Insurance Agent App harnesses the power of mobile conveniences to deliver better service, access, and communication to your customers. It's also the first mobile application to work with agency management systems, like QQ Solutions Catalyst. It can directly deliver policyholder's data (including POI ID's) into your customers' mobile devices.

Insurance Agent Apps' distribution system knows which customers install your agency's mobile application, how it's being used as well as allowing you to send push notifications to some or all of your customers who've installed the app. Additional features include a comprehensive accident report feature, bill pay, and a property inventory "app within the app" that expedites claims processing and reduces claims-related issues.

8

PAYMENTS KEEP YOUR CUSTOMERS

"Would you like to supersize that?"

"How about a new air filter with that oil change?"

"Would you like to make a donation to the local charity with your purchase today?"

When is the last time you paid for anything and weren't offered something more?

The reason almost every payment you make comes with an additional offer is because it works. Many people actually take the suggestion and end up spending more. For nearly every business outside of insurance, you only pay once each time you buy something. When you buy groceries, a meal at a restaurant, gasoline for your car, clothes – you get the idea.

I challenge you to name any other business that does not accept payments for the products they sell. I know you think insurance is different, and it is in many respects, but that won't keep your competition from allowing their customers to pay online.

If agents are as great at customer service as we think we are, then why aren't we offering our customers a solution to make payments, their most frequent interaction with us, easier?

Statistics show that customers will stay with an agency an average of eight years. During that time you will sell the policy once, it will renew seven times, endorsements will happen four times, and on average you will see about two claims. Do you know how many payment transactions will take place? During the eight years you have this client, you will have 80 payment transactions, making it your single highest -- and most valuable -- customer service interaction.

In fact, it's the transaction most likely to foster financial growth and success. What's unfortunate is that the bill received by your customer is often from the insurance carrier, not the agent who made the sale.

It's a basic truth that every solution to a problem tends to become a problem itself as time passes and things change. Before online payments came around, direct bill wasn't a bad thing for insurance agents. The American consumers' shift from physical payments to electronic payments has amounted to a plethora of missed opportunities.

The vast majority of your insurance customers have and will continue to pay electronically. The figure below helps drive home the point, showing the Federal Reserve Bank on non-cash payment trends.

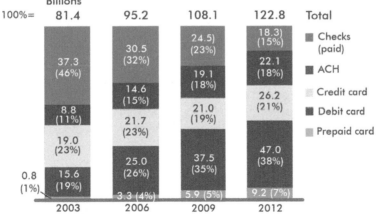

NONCASH PAYMENT TRANSACTIONS BY PAYMENT TYPE

Figures may not add due to rounding.
*CAGR is compound annual growth rate.
Source: Federal Reserve System

Though these statistics are important, they aren't the only reason why refusing to use payment processing is hurting your business.

1. You are losing website traffic, because your customers are going to your carrier payment page instead of yours.

2. You are losing out on cross and upselling opportunities.

3. You lose brand awareness to your carrier, because the customer interacts with them more than you.

I know a lot of agents have concerns about accepting payments, wondering, "Why should I take on more work? What if I get sued? Aren't credit card transactions expensive?"

Online payments aren't more work when your website is set-up to automatically process them, and it's worth it to ensure your customers are going to you instead of the carrier.

If you're concerned about a lawsuit, it's just an estoppel law issue. Estoppel occurs when you accept a payment for a policy that doesn't exist or isn't enforced. Accepting the payment creates the coverage. There are two solutions to this.

1. Your carriers pass the payment due information to your agency payment page. (This is the best solution, and you can help by encouraging your carriers to join the process.)

2. Your website only accepts "conditional payments." This is similar to when you find a payment slid

under your office door or a check in the mail. First you confirm the payment amount and acceptability. Then you deposit the check. A conditional payment allows your customer to request that you accept the payment, and it doesn't touch your customer's funds until you manually review the amount due and acceptability.

It's true that no agency can afford to pay three percent for a card payment when they're making a 15 percent commission. That three percent is 20 percent of the agency's total commission. The ideal solution is to remove that cost from the transaction, a strategy some companies have figured out. Although few are aware, there are now companies specific to the insurance industry that can process credit card payments without charging a fee.

The bottom line is that we need to stop giving away our best and most frequent customer contact point. Technology has transformed in a way that satisfies customers' enhanced expectations. It's time agents take advantage of that and take their customers back.

RESOURCES

Simply Easier Payments

Simply Easier Payments is a payment gateway created specifically for the insurance industry. It was designed from the ground up to be the only 100 percent legal solution that allows insurance agents to move the cost of the transaction from your agency to the customer making the payment.

Visa, MasterCard, Discover Card and American Express

49

have all acknowledged their method as compliant under their merchant contracts. Because the charge made by Simply Easier Payments is not a "convenience fee," this model is also allowed in the eleven states that have laws prohibiting these types of fees.

Hub2Pay, a service of Simply Easier Payments, is working to get your carriers to do this. The process is simple and is PCI Level 1, the highest possible Payment Card Industry Data Security Certification.

SECTION 2

"Agents can successfully counter the emerging perception of [insurance] as a commodity by 'going opposite' with their marketing strategy and fully embracing a local relationship-based strategy leveraging technology."

- Bob Rusbuldt, President & CEO

Independent Insurance Agents and Brokers of America

WEBSITE MOBILE

QUALIFYING	LEAD GENERATION	CONVERTING LEADS

QUALIFYING

BRANDING

USP

NICHE

LEAD GENERATION

ORGANIC

SEO

SOCIAL MEDIA

PROFESSIONAL LEADS

PAID

ONLINE ADVERTISEMENTS

COMPARISON LEAD GENERATORS

DIRECT MAIL

CONVERTING LEADS

SOCIAL MEDIA

CONTENT CREATION

EMAIL MARKETING

WEBSITE & LANDING PAGE

 OUTSOURCING

 AMS

RETENTION

QUOTING & CLOSING THE SALE

FILLABLE FORMS

DOCUMENT SHARING

TABLETS & MIRRORING

E - SIGNATURES

SMALL COMMERCIAL
LINES AUTOMATION

PERSONAL LINES RATING

ONBOARDING & SERVICING

WELCOME PACKET

EFT

CLIENT CERTIFICATE
SELF SERVICE

MOBILE APP

SELF PAYMENTS

EMAIL

SOCIAL MEDIA

CROSS SELLING & REFERRALS

SOCIAL MEDIA

EMAIL MARKETING

REFERRAL PROGRAMS

APP REMINDERS

TEXT MARKETING

9

QUALIFYING - TRANSFORMING THE TRADITIONAL SALES FUNNEL

Deploying your message through the appropriate communication channels is going to play a huge part in transforming your agency's marketing efforts. But first, let's dissect the traditional sales funnel.

You start out making cold calls to anyone with a pulse hoping your persistence will earn you some of their time. Then, you schedule a bunch of pointless meetings and quote anyone who allows it. Your final step is praying they take your offer. Sound familiar? It's totally backwards, and I have a pretty good idea of what happens next.

You soon learn the customer was just shopping, and you were just a commodity. You were used to either beat down their current agent, who they had no intention of leaving, or you were being leveraged against four other agents who were all saying the same prayer. You were a pawn in a game where the odds were stacked against you from the very beginning.

There's also the issue of actually obtaining a customer using this strategy. When you start the relationship this way, you're beginning at the bottom with an uphill climb. You may have got the business by some combination of perseverance, timing, pricing and a little bit of luck, which is all fine in principle. The diagram below shows what a traditional sales funnel looks like for most agents.

The only time you qualify prospects is at the end of the process, and your only barrier to entry is whether they will allow you to create a quote for them. Think about that for a minute. The only way you can qualify a good lead from a bad one is if they let you work up a quote.

The alternative to the traditional model, and the one you need to start using, is **qualifying** ideal customers right off the bat. When you do your qualification at the beginning of the marketing and sales process, it changes what the funnel looks like and greatly increases your profit per customer. The diagram below shows what the *Modern Customer Experience* funnel looks like.

WHERE QUALIFYING TAKES PLACE

MAKING CONTACT

SETTING THE APPOINTMENT

QUOTING

SALE

Both funnels start out equal in size and saturate the same amount of market share. However, the traditional funnel might look better because it stays wide throughout the entire process -- giving the illusion of more opportunities and money.

The difference between the two is that the sales funnel of the *Modern Customer Experience* gets smaller faster because your marketing and sales process is **qualifying** the perfect customer. This allows you to spend time and energy only on those you truly want to work with.

Here's a real world example to help explain. In the first funnel, you're a commercial insurance agent trying to write any business you can get your hands on. Since everything has an opportunity cost, and time is the most valuable asset we own, your time is worth $25 an hour ($50,000 a year). Then, let's say you do your prospecting based on the traditional sales model and make 100 phone calls.

Of those calls, you set 10 appointments and three ask for a quote. In the end, you lock in one customer. (Even though this is just an example, these numbers are generous.) If it took you 60 hours to make the calls, drive, hold appointments, work up quotes, present, etc., then it would cost $1,500 to acquire one customer that generates $2,000 a year ($10,000 - $15,000 for a premium account). Doesn't seem so bad.

Now let's apply the *Modern Customer Experience* model where you decide to only target construction contractors. You spend your time up front building your marketing and sales process so that only your best prospects are funneled down to you. Of course, you will still make updates to the system along with making some calls and appointments to further qualify your prospects.

Even so, this process only takes about 20 hours (compared to 60) with only five people (compared to 10) worth talking to, two of that five were worth quoting, and one becomes a final customer. It only cost us $500 (20 hours x $25 an hour) in time. Let's say we also spent $500 on marketing. Our total cost is $1,000 to acquire a $2,000 customer. We spent 75 percent less time and half the money for the same result.

Let's go one step further. Since we built a marketing system that runs on autopilot and continuously identifies and qualifies prospects, we now have way more time than we did before. We can accomplish in 20 hours what takes other agents 60.

Having additional time and money allows us to capture four times as many customers using the *Modern Customer Experience* model than it would using a traditional model. We can now acquire four new customers, which results in $8,000 in new revenue and only costs $2,000 ($500 x 4) to bring them on board.

Total, we made $6,000 ($8,000 - $2,000) in new revenue in the same amount of time it took the agent in the traditional model to make $500 ($2,000 - $1,500).

Note that your marketing costs will go down over time while your ROI increases. Once you build the snowball and let it roll down hill, it'll get bigger and result in a lower cost-per-customer acquisition. This system allows for organic growth in referrals and retention, which every agent wants, while doing away with cold calling, which every agent hates.

Another key takeaway is that we were able to increase our revenue through pointed marketing. Flip through your book of business and evaluate where you can make more money by identifying a profitable niche and building a campaign around it. If you're a commercial agent and you find that your best and most profitable customers are, indeed, construction contractors, shouldn't you be focusing your marketing efforts there? Or, if you're a personal lines agent and know your best customers are young families, tailor your efforts accordingly. Go after the groups that are the best fit for you and create the best opportunity for a substantial ROI.

Keep in mind that we all tend to buy from people we like or feel are similar to ourselves. Too many agents start out by, and some still do, throwing things at the wall to see what sticks. I'm not saying you shouldn't try new things, I believe quite the opposite. If you don't understand your purpose, vision, and strategy, you're going to just spin your wheels trying to get where you want to go.

To help you reach your goals quicker, you have to understand your branding message or Unique Selling Proposition (USP). Simply put, a USP is a statement that convinces someone they should buy from you. You'd be amazed at how few agents and agencies actually have one. Your USP should address these four statements:

59

1. I am (your professional identity)

2. I help (your target audience)

3. Do or understand (your unique solution)

4. So (your promised transformation)

Here is my USP:

"I am an insurance consultant who helps small businesses, specifically nonprofits, obtain the proper insurance. I do this by offering an insurance experience that few can. One that allows businesses to purchase, contact, and service themselves on their own time and how they want, so they can concentrate on growing their business instead."

If you're a new agent or just want to develop a niche for yourself, start by doing some research. Is there an underserved sector in your community? Is there something you enjoy, or a profession that you think would be interesting to do business with?

Once you determine the markets best suited for you, you'll have taken a huge step in creating a better customer experience. Your message and services will position you as a trusted advisor instead of a commodities broker. Here's a story to help drive home my point.

It was March 11, 2011, and I was at home on what seemed to be a normal day. The news was on and a story flashed across the screen. It was about one of the largest natural disasters in history, the earthquake and eventual tsunami that hit Japan. It was a tragic event. I immediately thought about the people in my own town and how important it is for them to have protection should something horrific ever occur in my area.

Giving your two cents on current events is a powerful tool for customer engagement. With Illinois as one of 16 states with the highest risk for earthquakes, I knew I should respond to what happened. I quickly grabbed my laptop and created a blog about earthquakes and separate deductibles. I then promoted it through a Facebook ad, and it became a hit for views and shares.

A gentleman in Oklahoma with family roots in my area happened to read the post and became a fan of my Facebook page. Over the next two years, he continued to follow my posts. When the time came for him to renew his insurance, he reached out. Turns out he was the vice president for an oil company and wanted me to take a look at his companies' insurance programs.

Initially, I said I would try and find someone else to help him out since I wasn't licensed in Oklahoma. That quickly changed when he sent me his dec sheets. After reviewing the size of the account, I decided it was in my best interest to become licensed in Oklahoma. In the end, I had a new customer that brought in $120,000 in premiums and $15,600 in revenue, all done on a broker of record. The amazing thing about this deal was that it was my marketing content and company branding that brought him to me. People should find you first, because those people are twice as likely to buy.

Everything you're struggling with, I've struggled with too. You may be lacking new leads and customers and think the issue is you're not working hard enough. I can only imagine how hard you work. That's not your problem.

The problem is that you're trying to dig a basement with a shovel when you really need a bulldozer. The laziest person in the world will move more dirt with a borrowed bulldozer than you can with your own shovel. This next section can be your bulldozer. Let's start moving some dirt.

Resources

Thomas H. Wetzel & Associates

Long-time insurance communicator, Tom Wetzel, (Rough Notes, Insurance Journal and social media guru) of Thomas H. Wetzel & Associates has created a great program for agents called *The Social Media Content Roadmap©*.

If you want your social media program to be a success, this is an invaluable tool for online marketing.

www.insuranceforeplay.com/tools

10

Lead Generation - With Little Time and Resources

Beginning in the 1800s, salespeople would go door-to-door pushing their products. They spent more time with prospective customers and built stronger relationships than we do today. Being in someone's home is a very personal thing. They had high closing ratios and limited expenses.

Then the telephone was invented and the prospect pool for most salespeople deepened. Agents were "dialing for dollars" and no longer needed to walk door-to-door. Taking the agent out of a customer's home drastically minimized personal relationships. Closing ratios fell (volume was used to make up for this) and expenses increased.

Today, our heads are spinning with the number of sales tools out there. The benefits of digital marketing are actually incredibly similar to that of door-to-door sales, but less than 20 percent of agents take advantage of it.

Digital marketing, like selling door-to-door, allows you to connect with customers in a more meaningful way. Closing ratios are higher and expenses dramatically decrease once you've established yourself.

With digital marketing and the *Modern Customer Experience*, you decide who you want to do business with. The best strategy is to have people find you first, because those people are twice as likely to become buyers. Instead of cold calling and prospecting, prove that you know how to solve a difficult problem and position yourself as an expert. Then replace manual labor with automation and your results will be dramatic.

There are two ways to generate leads, organically and paying for them. An example of using a paid lead is online advertising. Every time a customer clicks on your ad, you pay the platform where your ad lives (Google, for instance). Pay-per-click ads can be costly. However, if they're used correctly with thorough testing, they can make you a lot of money. Organic leads are obtained through your website, newsletter, or social media sites. What most people miss is that your organic leads can result from services people typically pay for.

ORGANIC LEADS

SEO

Did you know the word "insurance" has one of the highest search volumes on the Internet? Search Engine Optimization (SEO), in basic terms, is how well your prospects or customers can find you when they type in search criteria into a search engine. **It's anything and everything that helps your site get discovered and ranked in search engines — period.**

In the insurance industry, most agents have a terribly misconstrued view of SEO, because they've never taken the time to understand it. The problem for most agents is they don't have the money for optimal search rankings, or they're getting ripped off because they don't understand what they're paying for. All they know is someone promised they would get their company on the first page of Google.

SEO isn't just a singular thing, it's a process of elements that need to be executed on. Below are different marketing tools to strengthen your search ranking:

- Linking

- Blogging

- Sharing content on social media

- Verbally telling someone to go to your website

- Content marketing

- Facebook, LinkedIn and other social networking pages

Unless you have the money to burn, there is no easy solution for SEO. Search solutions are constantly changing, as are the chances of actually keeping your number one ranking.

The best way to build traffic and earn a top search ranking is to create useful content and share it with as many people as possible. Rinse and repeat. It means having a blog on your website that provides valuable posts and is SEO friendly. Google would rather see one quality blog per month than five that are dull.

Social Media

Social media is the ultimate networking platform. It's where people openly communicate and ask for advice on services and solutions.

Over time, social media can turn into a strategy for organic leads. Though I believe social media is better for converting leads (which we talk about more in the next chapter), it's still an important part of lead generation. Facebook has brought me leads simply through customers sharing my content and testimonials.

LinkedIn, the world's largest professional network, is great for commercial leads. It's become a search engine within itself for professionals looking for other professionals and has the additional benefit of helping people locate you on Google. The key to building a strong LinkedIn profile is focusing on the customer you're hoping to attract.

LinkedIn has the wonderful quality of being able to break down communication barriers too. I know agents who have tremendous success using the site to make introductions and set up meetings. One agent found about

75 percent of the people he contacts for meetings agree to get together with him because they're able to check out his credentials ahead of time.

Professional Leads

Connecting with professionals in other industries, such as real estate agents, bankers, accountants and car salespeople, who offer services that complement your own, can make for a mutually beneficial and profitable relationship.

The best agents who form these types of relationships have an incentive for the partnership. For instance, I created a referral program with local realtors from which we both benefit. They know I want the additional business, and I know they want to be compensated for giving me a referral. All I have to do is make it happen.

I pay for the realtors to get licensed as insurance agents along with a commission for the referral. They get renewal income for sending a new homebuyer to me, and I get leads I close 80 percent of the time that don't require additional work after the set up.

For my entire process, including the contract and spreadsheets I use to pay realtors, visit www.insuranceforeplay.com/resources.

PAID LEADS

Advertisements

Advertising only works if you know it's effective. No matter how large your audience is for traditional advertising channels such as print, radio and television, you have no convenient and concrete way to track if that's how you're customers are finding out about you. You're also charged for running the ad whether it's seen by 1000 people or 10, and it usually isn't cheap. With online advertising, you could run 50 ads at a fraction of the cost, see those that work, and continue to improve them for better results. You're only charged if someone actually clicks on the ad and you can specify the demographics you want to target. Online advertising is easily tracked with analytics available to fill you in on the who, what, where, when, and how of your ad.

For example, if you want, you can reach mothers between the ages of 30 and 40 who drive a minivan and watch Bravo. Or, you could run a LinkedIn ad specific to construction contractors in Green Bay, Wisconsin who bring in at least a million dollars in annual revenue.

Pretty incredible. Here are a few effective online platforms you can use to run your ads:

Facebook is great for generating leads, awareness and expanding your niche. You can be very detailed on the audience you want to reach. You can run ads displaying video, images or just text that are inserted into your audience's news feed or on the side in Facebook's dedicated advertising section. In addition, your ads can show up on mobile devices. More than one billion people access Facebook's mobile site per month.

The two reasons I run ads on Facebook are to drive people to my website or my business page on Facebook. Once your audience "likes" your Facebook page, you can start promoting your value so they think of you when they're ready to make a move.

LinkedIn ads are best for commercial agents targeting a specific professional or niche. As with Facebook ads, you can use images or text on LinkedIn. I would encourage you to use images in your advertisements. Forty percent of people respond better to content with visual elements than those with just plain text. Unlike Facebook though, videos are no longer supported on LinkedIn. Per their support page, "Advertisers can still add YouTube URLs to a Sponsored Update (paid post), which offers an effective way to drive engagement to your videos."

Keep in mind the ultimate goal of every advertisement is to drive people to your website.

Google Adwords was one of the first tools to effectively pair ads with the appropriate audience. If people are searching for "insurance" on Google, you can pay to position your ad as a search result.

These ads show up at the top or on the side of the search engine. Becoming proficient in Adwords, especially in a market like insurance, is no small feat. You can make a lot of money from the program, but you can spend a lot too.

Retargeting Ads work by keeping tabs on the people who visit your site and then redisplaying your advertisement on any others sites they visit. For example, if you go to a website that sells pots and pans and leave to visit a social media site like Facebook, you might notice their product ads on your page.

Retargeted ads can follow you to your inbox and other websites that allow it. When you add in the power of following people after they leave your site, you build true staying power with your prospects and customers.

Comparison Lead Generators

These programs give customers multiple options on a site to choose their insurance needs. Some comparison websites offer options for local insurance agents while others provide comparison pricing. Comparison sites work hard for top search rankings on Google and are quite effective for drawing in customers. Many times, a monthly fee is required to be listed on the sites.

Direct Mail

The marketing world can be cyclical. Direct mail marketing has once again become an effective form of lead generation with value add-ons such as personalization, a concept similar to online target marketing that allows you to choose to whom and where your message is going. As with any advertisement, incorporating strong imagery and a meaningful value statement will keep your dollars from going in the trash. Offline advertising, like direct mail, can also be used to drive people online.

No matter how you choose to drive people to your web or social sites, keep testing. Only trying one type of ad or marketing tool, and then giving up when you don't get the results you want, is an unfair assumption. It could be the wrong audience or the wrong message. Try a couple different options and really research what works before you dismiss online advertising altogether.

Resources

TrustedChoice.com

TrustedChoice.com was developed by the independent insurance industry and for the independent insurance industry, helping agents acquire quality leads through SEO.

Myself and many other agents get as many as ten leads or more a month, and it's not just personal lines. Agents are seeing leads in commercial lines as well. Tools like this one are going to save our industry. To learn more, check out www.trustedchoice.com.

www.insuranceforeplay.com/tools

11

CONVERTING LEADS -
FLIPPING THE SWITCH

In my first couple years of speaking, I felt like I was sending the right message but wasn't sure how my audience was receiving it or if they were actually doing anything with the advice I was giving them. Then one day, a veteran agent told me what he learned from my presentation, and it's a story I tell to this day. The conversation went something like this:

"Jason, this is the second time I've heard you speak. I have to admit, the first time I really didn't understand what you were trying to tell me. Today, I finally got it. I've been in this industry for a long time and heavily involved in the chamber of commerce, rotary club and other community organizations in my town. It was great when I started out, because it was the best way to meet new people. Lately I've recognized I'm not seeing any new faces. The people that belong to these organizations have been there for years, and I've done business with nearly all of them.

Every time I leave one of those meetings, I go home and tell my wife that if I could get everyone in my town to know me, like the people in those organizations do, I would have so much business coming through the door I wouldn't know what to do with it. Today, you showed me that by embracing technology, I can actually get everyone in my town to know me, just like they do in all of those organizations."

His story shows the real power of the online world. With traditional marketing channels, like newspaper or radio, we're told we have so many viewers, listeners, or subscribers, but there is no way to know for sure whose attention we actually have. So, we end up paying a bulk rate and may not really know how effective it was. With the way online marketing tools work today, you could run 50 ads at a fraction of the cost, see the ones that work, and continue to improve them for better results. If done properly, you can acquire leads while you sleep or spend time with your family.

Below are several social media platforms with details on how you can create a process that allows you to do more with less time, energy and resources.

Social Media

People don't want to feel like they're being sold. I once had an agent reach out to me who was having little success with his Facebook page for the past six months. He asked me to take a look at it, and after five seconds, I could tell exactly what he was doing wrong. Every other post was "get a quote from us" or "we have the best pricing in town." This type of blanket marketing will get you nowhere fast. It's also a good example of why the model outlined in the *Modern Customer Experience* funnel is effective. It narrows your prospect pool, so you can create niche-specific messages that will actually resonate with your audience.

The old adage, *"No one cares how much you know until they know how much you care,"* applies to social media too. While a site like Facebook can lead to sales, it's not a sales platform. It's for creating connections. Becoming great at social media takes time, patience, and creativity. Social content should be personal and informative. Build your posts around customer insights and needs, not your products and tactics. Once you get the foundation down for effective social marketing, it'll serve as a remarkably useful channel for you. Here's a rundown on how to use several of the social networks out there.

Facebook - Facebook works for acquiring personal and commercial lines customers, because people still buy from people. Once you setup your Facebook business page spend at least six months to a year doing nothing but building your audience by offering fun and informative content. Start by asking your Facebook friends to like your page and then ask them to have their friends like it too. Try running an ad as well to get targeted likes from people in your area.

After you've established a social media presence and a decent following, try running a contest to engage your followers. While requesting a quote from you isn't always top of mind, a contest with a great giveaway will stir some action. A 12-day contest that happens semiannually or quarterly is usually best. Prizes should be at least $100 in value. I've seen Kindles and iPads work very well.

The process you should use for ongoing social media success is what author and entrepreneur Gary Vaynerchuk calls the "jab, jab, right hook" strategy. The jabs are your content. The right hooks are things like contests and special offers.

Feel free to visit my Facebook page for live examples at www.facebook.com/jdcinsurance. If you're looking for specific social media strategies, like how to run a Facebook contest that can generate $40,000 in revenue in 12 days, go to www.insuranceforeplay.com/resources.

LinkedIn - LinkedIn is an online networking site for business professionals. On this platform, it's best to ask to connect with someone either right before or right after you meet them. Hosting or simply attending real world LinkedIn networking events is a wonderful way to help bridge the online and offline gap.

There are a few other things you can do to boost your business through LinkedIn. The first is to improve your profile. Your profile should read "this is the benefit you get from working with me" rather than "this is who I am and what I do." If you're a part of an agency, your organization should have its own page with an abundance of visual content and concise information.

Joining LinkedIn groups where potential customers might dwell is a valuable way to connect as well. Think of it similar to joining associations of the businesses you want to work with. These groups usually serve as forums for Q&As. Consider either starting or joining conversations.

LinkedIn, like Facebook, has a news feed that allows you to stream content. Repurpose your blog posts here with other original articles that cover trends and topics that establish you as a thought leader. Remember, everything you post should drive your business goals.

Google+ - Google+ is like a combination between LinkedIn and Facebook. It's more professional than Facebook but more casual than LinkedIn. Most importantly, it's owned by Google, and Google loves nothing more than when you use its stuff. While I wouldn't choose this as your go-to marketing tool, putting a little bit of time and energy into creating a Google+ page will help increase your local search visibility.

There are also great community groups on Google+, similar to those on LinkedIn, but with a slightly different audience. It's another chance for you to be a part of online forums where you can establish yourself as an authority on insurance topics.

YouTube - YouTube, a video sharing platform, is the second largest search engine and third most popular site on the Internet. It's also owned by Google. The best way to come up with content for YouTube is to think of the questions your customers want answered. Ryan Hanley, digital marketing lead at TrustedChoice.com, followed this strategy and created 100 videos in 100 days using only his smartphone. It led to a wealth of great content and customers.

+ **Pro Tip:**

If you upload your videos to YouTube before you post them on your other social sites, you'll get twice the

79

SEO juice.

If you want to learn how to set up your own video studio using only $250, visit www.insuranceforeplay.com/resources to get the info on all you'll need for free. It's a method I use along with TrustedChoice.com's Ryan Hanley.

Pinterest - As a discovery tool for projects and interests, Pinterest probably seems like an unlikely place to promote yourself and/or your business. However, in 2012, Pinterest became the second highest referrer of traffic to websites. Customers were ten percent more likely to buy if referred to a product through Pinterest. Its content is comprised mostly of images, giving you a chance to work your creative visual chops. Your blog, for example, should have bold graphics to complement content that can be used for pinning. In addition, ninety percent of the site's users are women -- something to keep in mind as you're drumming up content.

Over the last two to three years, Google has taken a substantial interest in Pinterest with some boards now claiming top search rankings on Google. To get your board one of those spots, create a title and description that uses keywords and consistently update your content.

The more popular your board is with pinners, the more popular it is with Google. As you build your number of followers, you can sprinkle in pins about what your agency is doing along with contests you're running.

For a deeper look at business for Pinterest, visit their resource center to help you properly set up your account at business.pinterest.com.

Content Creation

Creating valuable written content is like making an

investment that pays you dividends and returns forever. The only difference is you're making the investment in yourself and your business. Great content can benefit you for days, weeks, months and even years. It's your 24-7/365 salesperson.

The best content answers common or complicated customer questions such as:

- How can I save money?

- How can I add more profitability to my business?

- Do I have risks that could cost me money if not protected?

- Of the risks I have, how can I prevent them?

Your goal is to simplify the answer based on your expertise and knowledge. When you position yourself as an authority in your field, you're instilling confidence in your readers to look to you for advice.

In addition, content should be accompanied by a strong headline. It's the first thing people will read, and if it isn't compelling, it'll be the only thing. Eighty percent of people will read your headline but only 20 percent go on to read your content.

While blogs are the best place for sharable content, other avenues include books, articles, eBooks, white papers, diagnostics, or cheat sheets to name a few.

Email Marketing

The marketing channels mentioned above are even stronger when paired with an effective email marketing system. Email allows you to send your content right to your subscribers' inboxes without having to seek them out. Your campaigns can include things like a white paper or a link to a great blog post you wrote.

Email marketing is convenient too when you set up automations. An automation is a set of emails that go out whenever you choose to current or potential customers that opt in to your distribution list. For example, you might set up emails to go to a personal lines prospect once they opt in on your website or landing page.

Writing great emails is easier than you think. Just keep it simple, short and to the point. Emails should be formatted in plain text and written in the same tone you would use when talking with a friend. Think about the subject line in the same manner you would a headline for a blog post. Draw in the readers' attention without making outlandish claims. Subject lines are the most important part of your email. If no one opens it, the rest doesn't matter.

Finally, your emails should always have a call to action. What do you want your readers to do? Read a blog post? Ask for a quote? Think about what it is you're trying to accomplish and ease your intentions into the email. Remember, people don't like being sold.

Landing Pages

While you're probably familiar with websites, not many people have heard of a landing page. This is a page that serves as an extension of an advertisement or search result. It usually involves sales or promotional copy and might direct you to a business's social media site. People who land on the homepage of your website sought you out. People who end up on your landing page have no idea who you are. You need to convince them of your value. Offer visitors relevant and actionable content, such as an eBook or white paper. Then place them on an email campaign to stay connected.

Both a website and a landing page are important for your

overall marketing strategy although landing pages have a higher conversion rate. The most prominent feature on each should be the call to action, your opportunity to get your visitor to do what you want. What's your end goal? Supply a quote? Capture an email address? Use the landing page to place to execute your goal.

Rating Systems

The industry debate on rating seems to be evenly divided, but I've found it to be a very effective tool.

There's an agent on the east coast I've become acquainted with who does a great deal of business through his quoting system. Although nearly 50 percent of his visitors don't finish their quotes, his system alerts him even if just a small portion of information is entered. His team follows up within 15 minutes and ends up closing the sale about 80 percent of the time.

I think of rating systems to be similar to people raising their hands to tell you they're in the market to buy. If you don't give people the opportunity to ask for rates, you're turning your back on potential customers and giving your competition the chance to call them instead.

In summary, similar to how smartphones made us wonder how we ever operated before them, these incredible online tools make me wonder how we ever operated profitable agencies. Always remember this, these strategies require little setup with big results. Additionally, if you don't want to do everything yourself, there are companies in our industry who can affordably do it for you. Either way, don't wait any longer. The time to start is now.

www.insuranceforeplay.com/tools

12

QUOTING AND CLOSING THE SALE -

MORE SALES, LESS TIME

I once heard the CEO of a very large insurance company give a speech that was as blunt and direct of any I've ever heard. He was telling the audience what insurance companies really think about agents. *"We would get rid of you all tomorrow if we could. We just haven't figured out how to do it yet,"* he said. It's no secret some insurance companies are cutting commissions. There are even a few terminating contracts with agents. All of this is happening while the expenses required to run your business are escalating.

And so are customer expectations. Providing people with a quote in "15 minutes or less" has become synonymous with service standards. There's even an app out there right now that claims it can save drivers 30 percent or more in 30 seconds. At the bare minimum, both commercial and personal lines customers will soon expect a quote presentation once a year to make sure they're getting the best deal.

The good news is that technology advancements are available to significantly reduce the time, energy and resources put into the quoting process. Outlined below are several suggestions to effectively quote commercial and personal lines.

Commercial Lines Quoting Process

Most agents go directly to the client's location when beginning and finalizing the commercial insurance process. This is slowly changing, but still remains to be the primary way agents do business. I challenge you to look at video conferencing as an option. Like you, I initially thought there was no way someone would do business with me over a video conference. Boy was I wrong. I now have a few clients, as part of the onboarding service; I give a webcam and download Skype onto their computer. For the most part though, I go wherever my clients are.

So when you go out to your prospect's location to do the inspection, take your tablet or smartphone, capture pictures, and load them on to a platform like Google Drive or Dropbox. By using these platforms, your staff has access to them as well and can calculate a clear picture of the risk. Technology advancements will soon allow us to do everything from our office without going onsite, but for now, onsite is still needed.

When meeting with commercial client prospects, one option is to have the company's website up on your tablet and fill in the application questions while you're together. There are quite a few insurance underwriting departments that can get back to you in a few hours with a quote. After you're back from lunch with your prospect, your quote should be ready to go. Some departments even let you ask the questions, quote and bind right there.

Ideally, you should be pre-filling the application in your management system. But let's be frank, most of us just write down the information on a notepad. While it's nowhere close to ideal, it is realistic to what we do today. For those who don't do this, you can use my fillable forms that follow the ACORD forms. To access the fillable form I use for free, visit the resource section at www. insuranceforeplay.com/resources.

You, or your CSR, will put all relevant information together in an email and send it to the underwriters you want to work with. Finally, you receive the quote back from the company.

When you present to your prospect, bring two tablets, one for yourself and one for them. Open the proposal and use an app on your tablet that does what's known as "mirroring." This feature stops the prospect from going directly to the end of the presentation to see the price. Mirroring only allows the prospect to see what you want to show them, and goes through the presentation on their tablet at the same time you are going through it on yours. You could also do the presentation via conference call using Powerpoint or Prezi, eliminating the chance of the prospect going directly to the price. This method saves you a great deal of time, energy and money if the individual lives far away.

After you present, and the prospect likes your offer and price, go back to your office and put all the binding information into an e-signature service. The documents are then emailed to your prospect through encrypted email or an encrypted cloud. The prospect then signs the documents electronically, you are both emailed a copy, and you're ready to go with a new customer. E-Signature programs now have the ability to sync with certain agency management systems. Once the electronic document is signed by the new customer, it is automatically put into your system.

The insurance company you just bound the coverage with will do a digital download into your management system with all the customer's information. This eliminates a double entry for your new customer.

Leveraging technology the right way can be a great resource when it comes to renewal time for your customers. If you have the correct information in your agency management system, especially if you had the insurance company do a digital download, you can use a process called "bridging" to expedite the renewal process.

All you need to do is update some of the customer's pertinent information, such as changes in the risk, equipment, or employee changes that need to be noted. Once this is done you can electronically bridge (upload) the information over to the company. The insurance company can get a quote back to you much faster than they normally would, sometimes in half the time.

It's important to note that bridging technology has been around for almost 12 years. However, insurance companies are beginning to do away with it because agents aren't using it, and that's a shame. Most agents tried it many years ago when it was flawed. Now it works amazingly well. It just needs another shot.

(As a side note, we need to refrain from using the words "download" and "upload." We've used them in this book because that's the language some of you are familiar with, but they're now irrelevant in the context of sending an email. You're not going to say, "Hey I am going to upload an email to you. When can you download it back to me?" No, we say, "Hey, I sent you an email. When you've read through it, please reply.")

Bridging is very similar to the way agencies use download. Download is used 36 percent of the time for commercial lines. It's about 76 percent for personal lines. When commercial download first came out it was heavily flawed, but that's not the case anymore. Good management systems in conjunction with IVANS, ACT and carriers have fixed the problem.

Having walked in your shoes as an agency owner, and having talked and consulted with many other agency owners, it isn't hard to understand why many are resistant. You may have tried commercial download a while back and lost a lot of information in your system. You may be particularly sour about losing fields your employees customized and used for notes. It probably caused a major uproar with your staff leaving you hesitant to try it again.

Download is now a great tool and improvements are regularly added. The data in the management system is vital for all the other tools and workflows you need to provide a *Modern Customer Experience*. It's another sign that agents need to let go of the past. Things have changed. I know this from experience. Having been on the IVANS/Agents Advisory group representing management systems, I was involved in improving the delivery and accuracy of downloaded data. The industry is constantly working on process improvements, such as downloading documents as well as anything else you'd need from a company's website to add policy documents and notifications for claims and underwriting actions.

If you put your customer's information directly into your management system, bridging can be done on the front end of the quoting process. It can be a little tricky depending on your process and how many companies you want to send the quote to. However, there are a lot of companies that now offer bridging, and it will become commonplace in the very near future.

Personal Lines Quoting Process

The personal lines process is easy to break down, but the key to making your customers happy is keeping haste. Skip going to multiple companies that are going to slow you down, and you'll avoid hard costs associated with having to run MVRs and everything else it takes to do a solid quote.

Your first priority when setting up quotes for personal lines is to drive people to your website. Using the marketing tools and processes talked about in this book, you can create a program that sends leads to your site requesting quotes. Set up your quoting system to run on autopilot, and leads will automatically come in any time of day.

You will need to provide your leads with different options, such as:

- Allowing them to do the quote themselves.

- Calling you for the quote after accessing your contact information on your website.

- Create a fillable form on your website asking for basic contact information so you can reach out.

- Use a chat service to talk them through the quoting process.

As soon as you're notified someone visited your site and received a quote, follow up quickly to validate the information and close the sale. Statistics show with every minute that passes, your odds of gaining a new customer are significantly reduced.

Quoting systems exist to help collect leads for you, not to close the sale. That is still your job. As mentioned above, people have different preferences on how they want to receive a quote. Here's an example process used by the *Modern Customer Experience*.

A potential customer calls your agency asking for a quote. You bring up your online rating system and ask the required questions to give comparative rates. You then ask if your rates are competitive based on the person's current costs and coverages. If they are, let them know you're going to the insurance company with the best rate to lock in the prices.

Follow up by asking, "If this rate proves to be correct or better, do you want to go ahead with the policy?"

If they agree, gather the additional information you need and let them know it should only take five to ten minutes. Call them if any issues arise.

Once you've confirmed the price is good, call the customer back and let them know. Then, confirm their email address and tell them you will send binding documentation to be signed electronically. You then go to your e-signature program and upload all of your documents. Your next step is to email the documents off to your new customer. When your customer opens the email, they'll click a few buttons to sign the documents and finish. The e-signature system automatically sends the signed documentation to you and your new customer, and the process is complete.

By completing the entire personal lines process over the phone and online, you're separating yourself from the pack. You've also got a new customer that took little effort to acquire, and you spent next to nothing. More importantly, your new customer is happy because they now have an insurance policy that costs less and offers better coverage.

Most of us do these things in one way or another, but here a few things that'll bring you to the next level.

All downloads from the carrier to the AMS are done through "download codes." As the download comes through, these codes tell the AMS what type of download it is. For example, PCH is a policy change code or REN is a renewal code. Carriers and companies can have their own unique codes, but we're going to use these for the sake of this example.

The secret is that activities can be set based on those download codes. As the download comes through, you can tell the AMS to take specific actions per the code.

Let's say a client calls in and makes a change to their auto policy. They want to delete vehicle A and add vehicle B. The phone system the agent uses automatically detects the client through caller ID and opens the client in the AMS.

The CSR then clicks the realtime button in the client's folder for the auto policy. The AMS logs them into the company site and takes them right to the screen the CSR

93

CUSTOMER SERVICE IS JUST FOREPLAY

needs to enter their information to make this change. After entering the client's information, the CSR tells the client the difference in the premium and lets them know the ID card will be updated in their agency phone app within the next 15-30 minutes as well as emailed immediately.

The company then downloads the change into the management system. When the download code PCH (policy change) comes into the AMS, it triggers the pre-set activities you have set to happen when the AMS receives that PCH code

Here is an example of four activities that could be set to the example above:

Activity 1: Pre-fill out a specific document in the agency document library with the change information (vehicle deleted, the one added, the date of change, the premium increase or decrease and the new premium).

Activity 2: Pre-fill an ID card.

Activity 3: Send document and ID card to the client's email.

Activity 4: Send a notification to the agency app that the change was made.

You can use this system today. It's what your clients expect and want, and it'll set you apart from your competitors.

Tom Barrett from "Dynamics of Selling" expanded on customer service practices today, and I think the example he uses is fantastic. Tom explains there are four main factors in the sales and customer service process. Imagine each one of these factors as a card an agent keeps in his arsenal to use with customers.

The first card is price. Who controls the price? The insurance company. Agents have no say in coverage costs. They're all dictated by the company.

The second card is coverage. Who controls coverage? Again, this is the insurance company. They have total control over what coverages agents are permitted to offer.

The third card is service. Who controls service? For the most part, it's 20 percent the agent and 80 percent the company. While the agent may be the one customers interact with, the company controls every part of the service process. The only real service agents provide is billing and claims, even though the company still does both of those things.

The fourth card is relationship. Who controls the relationship? This is the agent's time to shine. You have full control from beginning to end.

Even though the company controls more than 70 percent of the sales and service process, don't let that discourage you. You can keep the service card in your deck by leveraging tools, such as mobile apps, e-signatures, social media, digital marketing and online payments, etc. If you mold an experience for your customers that allows them to do things their way and on their time, you're creating true value in the relationship. So when someone asks your customer who their insurance is through, they'll say your name instead of the insurance company's.

www.insuranceforeplay.com/tools

13

ONBOARDING AND SERVICING - SIMPLE AND PROFITABLE

What's the most important asset in your agency? Without a doubt, the answer should be your customer list. Given that, shouldn't you be dedicating a fair amount of time to building a process that accurately captures their information and ensures they're happy with you?

On my podcast I talked with an insurance agent in Washington who reaches out to her customers 18-20 times a year. That's pretty amazing. As a result, she has an unbelievably high retention rate and happy customers. This is what the *Modern Customer Experience* is about, making amazing a standard practice in your agency.

Another reason to have an effective agency management system is so you can properly catalog customer information and build a program around your value. Adding technology advancements to your business will serve you well. People are more inclined to use your programs if they're accessible on smartphones, tablets, and computers.

Before you move forward, make sure you have a process that verifies you're collecting and cataloging the correct client information. It's surprising how many agencies still don't ask for things like email and cell phone numbers, two of the most common ways to contact someone.

After you've gathered your customer's contact information, send them a welcome email and pack. It's not a common practice among insurance agents, which is all the more reason to do it. It's a good way to establish the foundation for a long-term relationship.

Your welcome email can easily be set to auto reply when a new customer is added to your AMS system. In addition, you can outsource your welcome pack to a printing company to make it easier for your agency to manage. In the future, agency management systems with an open source API will be able to automatically connect to your designated printing company and send out packets as new customers are added.

Welcome packets and emails should include:

- A thank you and welcome message.

- Contact information for your agency and the insurance company.

- Details on how to download your mobile app.

- Information on your agency's mission and community involvement.

- The different ways they can connect and communicate with you. (To welcome clients on social media, you could add them to your social network and send a message thanking them for their business.)

- The customer service options you provide, such as chat, email and phone.

- Let them know about any self-service programs you have, like payments and certificate management.

You should strive to get every new client setup on EFT, because it will save a lot of time and money for your customers down the road. For larger clients, most businesses have multiple **onboarding** calls or visits to their agency. Use this time to get them accustomed to your self-service options for payments and certificate management.

To be really great at retaining customers, especially your most profitable 20 percent, you must provide unmatched expertise. Getting together on renewal dates or when they have a problem won't be enough, even for personal lines customers. Step into your customer's shoes for a second. What are their biggest pains? The answer may vary depending on who the customer is and what they do, but for the most part, you'll find some common themes. For example, a business owner might be concerned about:

"What can I do to reduce my risk and claims to improve my loss ratio and decrease my premium amounts?"

"What tools are available to better train my employees so I have fewer worker's compensation claims and accidents?"

"As an insurance agent, what issues do you see that are effecting my business?"

If you leverage the tools and strategies discussed throughout this book, you'll give yourself more freedom to study and become an expert in your desired business niche. There are also programs like Real Time that agents can use to help increase efficiencies with normal servicing tasks.

Real Time is a national initiative that gives immediate access to carrier information on clients with the click of a button in your agency management system or comparative rater. The transaction may be a quote, billing inquiry, claim inquiry/loss runs, policy view, endorsements or a request for information. Real Time provides a single workflow for **servicing** or quoting.

It also straightens out the password nightmare and allows you to complete the tasks or services automatically. It's the autopilot of communication between your agency management system and the insurance companies' mainframe. It saves time and frustration. It also enhances the customer experience by operating simply and quickly.

The number of agencies using Real Time grows every year, along with the stories of saving time and money. According to Ron Berg, the executive director at ACT (Agents Council of Technology), Download saves around

81 minutes per employee every day. That's roughly 324 hours a year for each employee. If you're paying someone $15 an hour, that's $5,000 per employee that you're saving annually. To learn more about this free service, visit www.getrealtime.org.

Still, many agencies feel overwhelmed and can't seem to see through the weeds. Recent statistics show nearly 80 percent of the insurance industry is comprised of small agencies generating $500,000 or less in premiums. Leaner agencies mean agents need to think differently about how they get their work done. There are a number of companies out there, insurance or not, that can help you accomplish more and save more.

I can confidently say that agencies outsource to bring down operating costs. They also do it to use technology and resources more effectively in order to focus on servicing existing customers and leads. For the right kind of agency, outsourcing can do the following:

- Save on company capital

- Generate a variable cost arrangement

- Free up internal staff

- Generate more revenue

- Advance and enhance quality

- Cut your operating costs

By bringing in outside help, agencies are allowing themselves to build better and more profitable organizations. Outsourcing can help agencies with things like:

- Policy servicing

- Checking on policies

- Accounting related tasks

- Reporting related tasks

- Marketing

If you apply technology, outsourcing, and marketing tools correctly, you'll give the impression your service never quits. Ask yourself if you really have what it takes to be a trusted partner to your clients. If you can answer "yes," you've got the power to build a great business.

RESOURCES

Marble Box

When you begin outsourcing your back-end processing tasks, a company called Marble Box becomes an extension of your business. They work, and continue to work, while maintaining the uniqueness of your agency.

There are no hidden costs and you're given a dedicated team to take on the services you'd rather allocate to someone else. Their team is trained in your management system, while your in-house team spends less time worrying about everyday processing. In addition, your agents have more opportunities to offer clients, create more efficiencies, and increase the agency's revenue.

www.insuranceforeplay.com/tools

14

CROSS SELLING AND REFERRALS - AUTOMATED GROWTH

Any insurance agent will tell you referrals are an integral part of their business. We all know how rewarding it is to have a happy customer send one of their friends our way. It's the ultimate acknowledgement that your agency is doing something right. Your customer list is one of the most valuable assets you own. Not to mention, selling another product to a current customer is twice as easy as obtaining a new one.

Up until last year, I assumed referrals were no more than a byproduct of my usual process. That was until I did an interview with Chuck Blondino, director of marketing for Safeco Insurance, on my Agents Influence podcast. He brought up some staggering statistics on how agents are really bad at generating referrals.

He told me most agents only get about one out of 700 customers per month to give them a true referral. The top 25 percent of agents only get one out of 200 customers. The very best agents get one out of 85.

So how do agents receive quality referrals on a regular basis? I've had a lot of success with referrals using social media. I once had someone in my area post on Facebook they were looking for a great local agent. Five agents were suggested by those who answered the post. One was mentioned once, another was mentioned twice, a third was mentioned three times and the fourth was mentioned four times. The last agent was me. I was mentioned 18 times. Guess who that person ended up doing business with?

Insurance people....who has the best price for the best deal? Looking into switching our house, cars, and possibly life insurance over, ASAP!!

Like · Comment · Share

 Blake Perez Jason Jones farmers insurance here in Centralia saved me money. Run by his office and see. By the west side fire station where the ctb atm is located
Yesterday at 12:06pm via mobile · Like · 👍 1

 Maleah Sanders Oh ok. Thank you 😊
Yesterday at 12:06pm via mobile · Like · 👍 1

 Stacey Leonhardt Keef Jason Cass
Yesterday at 12:10pm via mobile · Unlike · 👍 5

 Chelsey Etheridge Davis Travis Etheridge
Yesterday at 12:14pm via mobile · Like · 👍 2

 Ashley Elizabeth Turczi Give Gene Odle a call Maleah Sanders he sells all types of insurances and can give u quotes on different ones that will meet ur needs
Yesterday at 12:14pm via mobile · Like

 Arica Basenberg Foltz I've told you several times. 😐
Yesterday at 12:14pm via mobile · Like · 👍 1

 Terri Kelly Travis Etheridge at Co. Mutual he is a really good agent!
Yesterday at 12:19pm · Like · 👍 2

 Kasei Cluck Kuhns I don't have them but I've always heard bean insurance in mt Vernon were really good on premiums!
Yesterday at 12:41pm via mobile · Like

 Danielle Hartrup Definitely Jason Cass!!
Yesterday at 1:05pm via mobile · Unlike · 👍 6

 Melodee Freels auto owners...Scott Alcorn
Yesterday at 1:05pm via mobile · Like · 👍 2

 Jamie Kelsheimer Cole We switched to Jason Cass & saved $$
Yesterday at 2:16pm via mobile · Unlike · 👍 4

 Steve Schwalm Jason Cass helped me
Yesterday at 3:17pm via mobile · Unlike · 👍 3

Though social media is great for referrals, it can be inconsistent and is only a piece of a larger puzzle. There are several other factors agents need to consider when automating their referral program.

I spent some time with the guys at Rocket Referrals and love some of the concepts they've come up with. Here's my take on referrals mixed in with their advice. I also have a great referral method in the resource center that any agency can apply to their business. You can access it by going to www.insuranceforeplay.com/resources and entering in your email address.

Miss Referrals, Miss Money

As important as referrals are, only elite agents have a comprehensive plan to get more. Too often agents' referral strategies begin and end with providing great service.

Earlier this year, management consulting firm, Bain & Company, released a study on customer loyalty in the P&C and life insurance market. Their research provided unique insight into how customer relationships play an important role in carrier and agency revenue growth. Bain concluded that, "While earning goodwill among customers is necessary, it is insufficient for generating superior revenue growth. Leaders must also motivate customers to actively promote the company." The responsibility is yours to inspire your customers to refer you, and you inspire them with a great customer experience.

Think of customer satisfaction as a prerequisite to customer loyalty. Do whatever it takes to make your customers happy and make sure they can't stop talking about you. That's how referrals are created.

Think Differently About Referrals

Your strategy to increase referrals needs to begin with your agency's mindset. Every interaction you have with your customers should make them want to suggest you to others. This includes everything from how you communicate down to the subtleties in your language.

Most importantly, you need to know why customers refer their friends and family to you. They certainly aren't concerned about adding profits to your bottom line. They do care, however, about improving the lives of their loved ones.

Make your customers feel like they're a part of a growing community or family. Keeping it personal and exclusive will ignite their emotional spark plugs and motivate them to actively refer you. Make your customers feel like you want to take extra special care of their friends and family. Remember, it's about them. Try sending a welcome card using language that conveys the significance of referrals to your agency.

Some effective ways of communicating with your customers about referrals might include:

"Taking wonderful care of you, your family, and your friends is what we love to do. Taking care of your insurance needs is what our office is all about."

"We would like to help even more people in the community feel secure with their insurance. The best way to do that is to get the word out. Please do not hesitate to share your experience with your loved ones. We love to help!"

Words have a lot of power. While your tactics may not work with every customer, most of them will be affected in a positive way.

Asking Doesn't Really Matter

There is an overwhelming misconception that asking for referrals will produce positive results. Research shows that asking is actually remarkably ineffective in the long run. That's good news for agents, because asking a customer for a referral is about as awkward as your Uncle Steve's whiskey-sprinkled wedding speech.

The most effective referral strategies don't involve actually asking for them. An Advisor Impact study focused on customer loyalty surveyed over 1,000 customers on why they refer a service to others. Ninety-eight percent said it was to help their friends and family. Only two percent said they did it because the business asked them to.

Effective referral marketing means identifying your loyal customers and sending them targeted messages that encourage referrals to their friends and family. Focus on finding your best customers and putting in the extra effort so they'll vouch for you.

Get the Best, Forget the Rest

So who are your best customers? There's an easy way to identify them. It's called the Net Promoter Score (NPS). This industry-recognized method is used by many of the nation's top companies, including Apple and Southwest, to gauge customers' willingness to recommend. The NPS is particularly useful for insurance agents because of our ability to establish personal relationships. In short, the NPS is a single question you can send out in the body of an email.

"How likely is it that you would recommend X agency to a friend or colleague?"

That's it. Lead with anything more and your response rate will drop significantly. Customers responding from 0-6 are classified as detractors, 7-8 are neutral, and 9-10 are promoters. An inexpensive way to send these surveys out is through Google Drive's form function. It's free and easy to use.

Make sure you ask a follow up question so your customer can explain their response. It's a great opportunity to collect testimonials or allow disgruntled customers to vent. Your email subject line should indicate you're only asking for a brief moment of their time. Email open rates are as high as 50 percent with something like, "John, two questions for you."

From: Jurgens Insurance <info@jurgensinsurance.com>

Subject: John, two questions for you.

Hi John,

It's important for my team and I at Jurgens Insurance to continue
making improvements. That's why I'm sending this email; to ask
you for your feedback. Your feedback will help us continue to
improve and offer the best service possible to you and others.

I only have two questions, and should take less than a minute to
answer. The first one is below, and then a second will open after
you click your response.

**How likely is it that you would recommend Jurgens Insurance
to a friend or colleague?**

0   1   2   3   4   5   6   7   8   9   10
Not Likely   Very Likely

Thanks so much! And as always if you need anything or have
further comments please call or email.

Jurgens Insurance
600 Mulberry St
Des Moines, IA 50309

The results will allow you to segment your customers
based on their willingness to refer. It goes without saying
that if your customers respond negatively to the NPS, you
should follow-up immediately. This works wonders with
customer retention. People like to know you care. The
majority of your focus, however, will be on the promoters
(those scoring 9-10).

Touch Them in All the Right Ways

Now it's time to take action and inspire your promoters to refer you. Begin with your best promoters, the 10s, and work your way down. This strategy gives you the biggest bang for your buck, because you can initiate quality communication and remain cost-effective. Your message should let them know you appreciate referrals, and you're eager to help their friends and family. Stay away from statements like, "Please refer me to your friends."

Every touch point with your customers plays a huge role in reinforcing your brand's image. It will also keep you fresh in your customers' minds. Consistently remind them that you're diligently working on their behalf with their best interests at heart.

Send Something Significant

The following types of communication are proven to be the most effective at bringing in positive recommendations.

Introductory email

Immediately after you acquire a new customer, send them an email that outlines your services as well as:

- Briefly thanking them for their business. Let them know you appreciate them.

- A list with the products you offer.

- A link to your website with additional information regarding your business.

- A phone number and email address. Encourage them to call.

- Encouraging them to forward the email to others

that might be interested in your services.

- Recommending they archive the email so they can reference it later.

- Making sure the email is from you. Don't use a template. If they reply, you should be able to respond directly.

Sending this type of content to your customer's inbox will make it easy for them to pick up their smartphone and forward it to those they want to refer. It's sort of like a virtual business card. It provides all the basics on your products and services, links for those that want to dig deeper, and contact information so you can be reached.

Welcome card

Research shows new customers are eager to refer products and services. Socially, it helps them validate their decision and fit in with peers. Keep the excitement going and squeeze out as many referrals as you can.

Inspire your customers to talk about you. Consider mailing a handwritten welcome card a week after they sign up to create a positive and lasting impact. It's a conversation starter that will linger on their kitchen counter.

Francis,

We are thrilled to welcome you to JDC Insurance Group! I truly enjoy sharing my experience with you and others. If your friends and family ever have questions or need advice have them call me directly. I'll take extra care.

Jason Cass 618.5322277 x 1

Loyalty card

Telling your best customers that you appreciate their business is very powerful. Loyalty cards are simple, handwritten notes that say thanks and remind customers that you offer other services should they ever require them. Because you're only sending this type of card to your most loyal customers, you can fit this strategy into your time and budget. They're also a great way to develop trust. Below is an example of a note I send to my customers.

Francis,

Thank you for being a loyal client. I value having you as a part of the JDC Insurance Group family. If you have any questions about your existing policy or are considering any other types of coverage just give us a call or send a quick email.

Jason Cass 618.532.2277 x 1

Thank you card

Referrals are a sincere compliment, and it's critical to thank your sources. Customers that have already referred you once are 20 times more likely to refer you than your average Joe.

Keep the fire going by letting them know you genuinely treasure their referral and will take care of their friends. Make them feel like they just contributed to your "family" of customers and welcome them to your team.

Francis,

Your referral means the world to us. We're honored that you entrust us with your friends and family. We will take extra care of Penelope!

Thanks so much,

Jason Cass 618.532.2277 x 1

Turning Out Testimonials is Gold

There are benefits of actively collecting testimonials that go beyond promoting your agency. Testimonials are also very effective for referrals.

Our brains use all kinds of tricks and shortcuts to help us make decisions quickly. One of those shortcuts is that people make decisions faster when a similar decision has been made in the past. Another is that we're consistent with prior decisions, especially when we've made it publicly known how we feel.

So what does all of this have to do with referrals? When someone publicly shares how they feel about your agency, they're much more likely to share that with their friends. You are essentially giving them an opportunity to practice a pitch they'll give on your behalf. As a bonus, the people that provide you with a testimonial are much more likely to become long-term customers because they see it as being consistent with what they once said.

Follow up the NPS survey by asking your promoters to provide you with a testimonial. Ask for a specific example where you've helped them. Your goal is to have your customer write a brief story about your service that highlights your strengths. That's what will resonate with prospects.

Follow the Money

Finally, it's important to stay on top of your referral sources and progress. Like any other area in your agency, a referral strategy should be consistent and tracked over time. Keep a list of the customers willing to recommend you and the efforts you've taken to communicate with them. Log the success of your strategy and adjust it over time.

Maybe you're already asking new customers how they heard about you. If you use this method, you'll receive mostly generic responses like "Google" or "a friend." That does nothing to strengthen your referral strategy or thank your active promoters. Instead, consider asking every new customer who referred them to you and that you'd like to send them a thank you. This question is much more explicit and yields more precise information to help you better identify your active promoters.

Resources

Rocket Referrals

Implementing the practices above will help you create a steady referral process for you and your agency. However, if you're like me and already very busy, find a company that will do the work for you.

Rocket Referrals brings me testimonials, referrals and improves my customer retention. The cards you previously saw in this chapter were automatically developed and delivered in my own handwriting by Rocket Referrals to my best referral sources. They have patented handwriting and printing technology that makes them an amazing resource and alleviates the additional workload of having to manage everything myself.

15

The Modern Customer Experience -

MAKE IT YOUR OWN

Remember at the beginning of the book where the McKinsey & Company report made a comparison between insurance agents and travel agents? Let's look at that again and dig deeper into what separated the travel agents that survived from those that did not.

As mentioned earlier, travel sites like Orbitz and Expedia entered the marketplace and wiped out travel agencies' market share. These sites made it incredibly simple for people to book their plans online, similar to what your competitors are doing to you right now. Although this meant the end for many agencies, those that adapted and focused solely on specialized travel outside of the U.S. created a better and more profitable business for themselves.

This book can help you and your agency survive if you're willing to transform. So, where do you start? It's a tough question to answer, because every agency has a different problem to solve. Unfortunately, this book doesn't have a magic genie who will do everything for you. That's just not how the world works, and it certainly isn't how implementing the *Modern Customer Experience* works either.

Use this book as a guide. Ask yourself some tough questions about your agency and the future. Keep this book by your side over the next couple of years, take notes in it and join our online community. Stay up to date on future resources by going to www.insuranceforeplay. com/resources and entering your email address. Your goal should be to take one or two things now, those golden nuggets for you and you alone, apply them and see them through to completion.

To help you build the *Modern Customer Experience* for your agency, I have provided two guides. Remember, no two agents are alike. Take this information and use it in a way that works best for you.

First, here is a list of steps I encourage you to take to build your *Modern Customer Experience* and a more affluent agency. These steps, along with the infographic we provided for you, will serve as a guide as you go through your own internal process.

1. Get an Agile Agency Management System

An Agency Management System is like the spoke in the wheel that runs your agency. It should connect to the systems and tools you're using to make life easier. This is easily one of your biggest leverage points for exponential growth.

Start by taking a good look at your agency's management system or setting one up if you haven't yet. Too many agents are using systems that are outdated and a bad fit for their agency. Getting started is never easy, but the convenience it will afford you will be worth the initial work.

2. Build a New Website That Sells

Your website really is your virtual storefront. It's where people make the decision whether or not they want to do business with you. Keep your website up-to-date and modern because people are judging you by your cover. So what does your website, or lack of one, say about you?

When building or revamping your website, focus on making it easy to navigate, ensuring it's SEO friendly, prominently displaying your contact information, incorporating a strong call to action, utilizing social media buttons, implementing a blog and optimizing it for mobile devices. It should be one of your best sales tools.

3. Give Your Customers Self Service

Time is money. How are you spending your time? Improving your internal operations is one of the quickest

123

ways to reduce expenses and add to your bottom line. As insurance companies continue to reduce commissions, this will become even more important.

Work on things like improving the quoting process, offering self-service, delivering risk management solutions and small commercial and personal lines quoting software. In addition, one of the best ways to create efficiencies is to offer a payment system that allows your customers to pay their insurance premiums through you. This strengthens their relationship with you instead of the insurance companies.

4. Embrace Mobile Technology

We live in a mobile society. You should have a mobile friendly website in addition to a mobile application. Be sure you create "mobile moments" for your customers and offer features such mobile payments, access to ID cards or the ability to make policy changes.

5. Use a Real Referral System

Your customer list is your most valuable asset. You should be maximizing and leveraging it all the time. A great referral system not only gets you quality customers from your current customers, it also strengthens your customer relationships. Every time they refer someone to your agency, they're reinforcing how happy they are to be your customer.

Every agent, including myself, loves to think we do a great job with referrals, but we don't. Most start out with the best intentions and slowly fade to nothing. Build an automated system that requires as little involvement from you as possible.

6. Establish Your Brand Message and USP (Unique Selling Proposition)

Figure out the purpose of your brand and the direction you want to go. Your brand message and Unique Selling Proposition will bleed into so many other areas once you do.

Talk to your customers to find out what they need, what you can offer them, and why they think you're better than the next guy. You may also want to brainstorm with your team or a consultant to help develop your brand. Whatever you come up with, let's hope it's better than "we offer the best customer service." Even if you really do offer the best, put a different spin on it. Give your customers a message that resonates.

7. Develop Your Marketing Funnel

Even though I speak a lot about marketing, and believe it's extremely important, it doesn't mean much if you don't have the other items on this list checked off. Once you've done that, dive into your marketing system and sales funnel.

Utilizing technology like social media, online advertising and email marketing will help you access a new demographic of buyers. Also, if set up correctly and connected to your Agency Management System, referral program, and other tools, it'll help your sales funnel grow effortlessly.

8. Bring It All Together - Retention & Cross Selling

Every piece of your agency should work like a fine-tuned machine. At least that's what every agent wants. A good question to ask yourself is, "Am I busy getting after my work or am I just working to stay busy?"

The right tools and digital marketing methods can give you freedom to do the things that mean the most to your customers. In return, it will all lead to better retention, cross-selling and sales.

Second, here is what the *Modern Customer Experience* might look like on any given day:

Generate quality leads. There are a lot of ways to do this. If you use the best tools available, potential customers should find your company online. For instance:

- They use Google to search terms like "construction insurance" or "car insurance." With the right SEO strategy, you'll come up as one of the top search results. They can then click the link that will take them to your website.

- They may read a testimonial on Facebook from one of your clients, reference you when a friend is asking for help with insurance, or read a blog post you wrote that someone in your community is sharing. That person then clicks on the blog share button and goes to your website.

- One of your professional leads, such as a real estate agent, connects you with someone on LinkedIn or Facebook that they think would be a good client for you.

- A potential customer clicks on one of your targeted social media or Google ads that takes them directly to your website.

- They access a comparison lead generator, such as TrustedChoice.com, through a search engine and find your name as one of the listed providers in their area.

Convert leads into prospects. If you use any of the methods listed above for generating leads, you're going to want to drive the lead to your website, blog (on your website usually), landing page or social media page. After

126

this happens, there are a number of steps that can help convert the lead into a prospect. Again, these can all be set up on autopilot for you and your agency.

- To get a better idea if they want to do business with you, a customer might ask to connect on one of your social networks to learn more about you and what you do for the community, etc.

- They read a post on your blog about an issue they may have experienced that solidifies your position as an industry expert. Once they trust your advice, they may go on to read your other posts and check out your website for additional information.

  · They go to your website and sign up for your email list to either be notified of future blog posts or to access a white paper or eBook you wrote. Once you've captured their email, you can drip market content that may eventually convert this person into a potential customer.

Quoting and closing prospects. As mentioned in the chapter on quoting and closing the sale, technology can greatly increase your profitability and reduce the time and energy you're exerting into your business. Using processes and tools like fillable forms, document sharing, tablets, mirroring apps, and e-signatures will help you get more done with less.

- Be sure to utilize your agency management system to improve your efficiencies and make more money throughout this process.

- People expect to be able to get a quote when they visit your website. Using personal lines and small commercial rating systems will help give them what they want while allowing you to qualify leads with a hands-off approach.

Onboarding and servicing new clients. Onboarding

a new client should involve more than it currently does for most agencies. Bringing on a new client should mean creating a great first impression. Let them know you'll operate in whatever ways that work best for them. Make sure your team is collecting all of your new client's information like email, a cell number and the way they prefer to be communicated with. Using technology and a simplified process will ensure nothing is missed. In the end, you'll create value with your clients and profitability for your agency. Some of your go-to tools should be:

- Email marketing

- Welcome packet

- Mobile app

- EFT

- Self Service

  · Certificates

  · Payments

  · Risk Management

- Real Time

Cross selling and referrals. As the consumer continues to expect more for less, having a broader reach while doing less will become increasingly important. Leveraging social media, email marketing and other new and developing technology to increase cross-selling and referrals will be crucial to your success.

- Unless you are naturally great at getting referrals, which most agencies aren't, you need to build a process that ensures it automatically gets done internally. If you don't have the time, get outside help. Current customers are the best way to get new ones.

128

- Use the tools to send your clients reminders and information that is valuable to them. This, of course, can be done by email or social media. Other options are your agency app and text message marketing. Either one, if done correctly, will let you inform clients of payments due or changes to their policies.

Your future in this industry can be a bright one and it should be. It has never been easier to create and build a successful business than it is today. The technology and creativity we have access to lets you manage systems that will actually do most of your work for you.

In Jim Collins's book, *Great By Choice*, he talks about two camps of hikers that set out on a 1,400 mile trek (equivalent of New York to Chicago and back) in an environment that was 20 degrees below Fahrenheit. They had no form of modern communication and being rescued was unlikely if something went wrong.

Collins talks about how one camp would drive themselves to exhaustion if the weather was good but wouldn't hike at all on the days the weather was bad. In contrast, the other team would do no more than 20 miles a day no matter rain or shine. They never went further than 20 miles, even on nice days, and always kept moving no matter how bad the conditions were.

Long story short, the team that did just 20 miles a day completed the trip in less time than any other group and with the entire team still in good form. The other group that was erratic in their approach never made it to the end and many members of the team even died. The takeaway is that you need to create your own 20 mile march, a conscious decision of what you are going to do to get better, and then implement a part of that strategy every single day.

About the Author

Jason Cass

Jason is a thought leader, speaker, agency owner and champion for the independent insurance industry. His agency, JDC Insurance Group, is located in southern Illinois. Over a few short years, Jason built a profitable agency that can be run virtually and digitally. He is almost 98.9 percent paperless and owns no filing cabinets.

His CSR lives in Georgetown, Colorado, 984 miles from his home in Centralia. All backend work is done in India. The agency is comprised of 75 percent commercial lines, 20 percent personal lines and five percent life. Ninety-eight percent of his customers pay EFT. Over the last few years, he's spent $6,942 on marketing to generate more than $204,200 annually for his agency.

Because of Jason's success, he's served as Chairman of the National Young Agents committee for the Big I for several years. He averages more than 20 speaking engagements a year for associations, insurance companies and vendor events across the country.

Through speaking engagements, along with his involvement in the Big I, he's been able to really understand what's going on in insurance. Jason has addressed thousands of agents, CEOs and industry thought-leaders to gather insights. This book is a culmination of the information he's acquired through each of his experiences.

Jason now owns the GROW Program which helps agents discover and implement their online social and digital strategies. At GROW, they offer online educational programs in digital marketing called DIMA (Digital Insurance Marketing Academy) and run an online mastermind group for agents. He also has a podcast called "Agents Influence" where he discusses the biggest issues affecting the industry from an agent's perspective. (www.agentsinfluence.com)

Jason is happily married to Andrea Cass. They have two sons, Gavin and Rylan.

About the Writer

Brian Appleton

Brian is passionate about building communities, developing organizations and enhancing company cultures. He writes and speaks about insurance, sales and personal development. His first six years in the professional world were spent at one of the 100 largest insurance agencies in the country. He eventually partnered with Jason to help build the GROW Program.

After two years building GROW, Brian shifted his focus to content creation, writing and self-publishing both for and outside of the insurance industry. In addition, he works with technology startups that build tools for the insurance industry such as the mobile employee training company, Inside Out LMS.

Brian graduated from the University of Iowa with a degree in finance and risk management and insurance and currently lives in Des Moines, IA. You can reach him at brian@insuranceforeplay.com.

ARE YOU READY
TO GIVE A
MODERN CUSTOMER
EXPERIENCE?

Top 3 Improvements to Make

☐ _____

☐ _____

☐ _____

☐ *Get Resources*

www.insuranceforeplay.com/resources

☐ *Get Tools*

www.insuranceforeplay.com/tools

☐ *Create a Modern Customer Experience*

www.insuranceforeplay.com

CPSIA information can be obtained at www.ICGtesting.com
Printed in the USA
BVOW07s1202030116

431630BV00023B/135/P